FOUL DEEDS AND SUSPICIOUS DEATHS AROUND SOUTHPORT

TRUE CRIME FROM WHARNCLIFFE

Foul Deeds and Suspicious Deaths Series

Barking, Dagenham & Chadwell Heath
Barnsley
Bath
Bedford
Birmingham
More Foul Deeds Birmingham
Black Country
Blackburn and Hyndburn
Bolton
Bradford
Brighton
Bristol
Cambridge
Carlisle
Chesterfield
More Foul Deeds Chesterfield
Colchester
Coventry
Croydon
Derby
Durham
Ealing
Folkstone and Dover
Grimsby
Guernsey
Guildford
Halifax
Hampstead, Holborn and St Pancras

Huddersfield
Hull
Leeds
Leicester
Lewisham and Deptford
Liverpool
London's East End
London's West End
Manchester
Mansfield
More Foul Deeds Wakefield
Newcastle
Newport
Norfolk
Northampton
Nottingham
Oxfordshire
Pontefract and Castleford
Portsmouth
Rotherham
Scunthorpe
Southend-on-Sea
Staffordshire and the Potteries
Stratford and South Warwickshire
Tees
Warwickshire
Wigan
York

OTHER TRUE CRIME BOOKS FROM WHARNCLIFFE

A-Z of London Murders
A-Z of Yorkshire Murders
Black Barnsley
Brighton Crime and Vice 1800-2000
Durham Executions
Essex Murders
Executions & Hangings in Newcastle
  and Morpeth

Norfolk Mayhem and Murder
Norwich Murders
Strangeways Hanged
Unsolved Murders in Victorian &
  Edwardian London
Unsolved Norfolk Murders
Unsolved Yorkshire Murders
Yorkshire's Murderous Women

Please contact us via any of the methods below for more information
or a catalogue
WHARNCLIFFE BOOKS
47 Church Street, Barnsley, South Yorkshire, S70 2AS
Tel: 01226 734555 • 734222 • Fax: 01226 734438
email: enquiries@pen-and-sword.co.uk
website: www.wharncliffebooks.co.uk

Foul Deeds & Suspicious Deaths Around
SOUTHPORT

Geoff Wright

Wharncliffe Books

First Published in Great Britain in 2008 by
Wharncliffe Books
an imprint of
Pen and Sword Books Limited,
47 Church Street, Barnsley,
South Yorkshire. S70 2AS

Copyright © Geoff Wright, 2008

ISBN: 978 1 845630 61 4

The right of Geoff Wright to be identified as
author of this work has been asserted by him
in accordance with the Copyright, Designs and Patents Act, 1988.

A CIP catalogue record of this book is available from the
British Library.

Typeset in Plantin and Benguiat by
Pen and Sword Books Ltd

Printed in the United Kingdom by
Biddles

Pen & Sword Books Ltd incorporates the imprints of
Pen & Sword Aviation, Pen & Sword Maritime,
Pen & Sword Military, Wharncliffe Local History, Pen & Sword Select,
Pen & Sword Military Classics, Leo Cooper, Remember When, Seaforth Publishing
and Frontline Publishing

For a complete list of Pen & Sword titles please contact:
PEN & SWORD BOOKS LIMITED
47 Church Street, Barnsley, South Yorkshire, S70 2AS, England.
E-mail: enquiries@pen-and-sword.co.uk
Website: www.pen-and-sword.co.uk

Contents

Acknowledgements

We would particularly like to thank Matthew Tinker and his team in the Reference Department of the Atkinson Library, Southport, and Sam Cookson (photographs) for their assistance in this publication.

Also, the *Southport Visiter*, *Southport Champion*, *Daily Post*, Cedric Greenwood, Stephen Copnall and southportgb.com.

Lord Street West and the memorial lamp to the 'founder of Southport', William 'Duke' Sutton. Author's collection

Introduction

Ever since Cain slew Abel, the murder of a fellow human being has been regarded, in all societies, as a crime of exceptional horror. For what reasons have men – and women too – steeled their hearts and subdued their normal human instincts in order to commit what Shakespeare called 'that bloody sin ... murder most foul.'?

Man kills another for many reasons, but the two most common motives are greed and lust; they often involve money or sex – tending to be the ugliest of all - and both impulses can drive the slayer to insane lengths.

Murder provokes revulsion and fascination in most of us; it is an emotive and controversial subject, but sadly one that has always been part of the fabric of our lives, however abhorrent. To kill someone is the ultimate taboo; and that is why it scares us, but intrigues us too!

Millions of us regularly watch detective programmes and *Crimewatch*, or enjoy a good read about a classic old murder case, but of course we are purely on the outside looking in. The thought that it may happen one day to one of our loved ones, for example, does not bear thinking about. To take the life of an innocent woman or child in particular, is inexcusable and impossible to comprehend.

Southport Visiter's *Crimefile logo*. Southport Visitor

It is a sad fact that the younger members of our society are just as likely to suffer death at the hands of unstable people. The worst case scenario was the chilling case of little Amanda Graham who joyously went with an older friend to the fairground one summer's day in 1961 – only to be abducted, taken to *Birkdale's Grand Palace Hotel*, never to return home.

Although this quiet pocket of Lancashire may not have been home to notorious crimes, it has been the location of a couple of notable cases, including that of 'doctor death' and the 'case of the century', when Robert George Clements was charged in 1947 with

A good early beach scene. Author's collection

poisoning his fourth wife, and strongly suspected of doing the same with the others.

There is also the baffling murder of a respected businessman, Harry Baker, in 1958, who was found stuffed into two coal sacks in an isolated field; the unsolved murder of the thirty-one-year-old gay shop owner Nigel Bostock in 1986; the double-slaying of two friends by evil bouncers, and of course the chilling murder and aftermath of Lynsey Quy – the worst murder story in Southport's history.

Further murderous stories include: a fatal brawl at the

A judge dealing with a foul deed. Author's collection

Shakespeare pub; the strangling of religious zealot the 'Pink Lady'; the plundered moneylender; and the woman murdered by her sex-starved husband.

Each case has its own affecting points of interest, running the gamut of every human emotion. A second book will appear next year, which will include some more nineteenth century murders.

All these macabre tales help complete this first collection of stories from the darker side of the 'sleepy' holiday resort of Southport. But as they said on *Crimewatch* after reporting on the dear old mugged granny 'don't have nightmares, sleep well'.

Southport Infirmary, Scarisbrick New Road. Author's collection

A Wolseley utilised as a police car in 1930s Southport. Author's collection

An 1870s policeman.
Author's collection

A 1931 patrol car. Author's collection

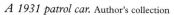

Chapter 1

Pub Brawl at *The Shake*
Shakespeare Hotel
1870

A lesson for all those a bit too quick with their fists. A fatality took place outside the Shakespeare Hotel, *on Scarisbrick New Road when, during a drunken brawl, 'the loser' was knocked to the ground, hit his head on to the curbstone - and was picked up dead!*

Less than 100 yards from his home, there was 'Much Ado' about something when Thomas Greenwood's local pub, the *Shakespeare Hotel*, hit the headlines when a fatal fight took place just outside on the Scarisbrick New Road corner, on Saturday, 16 July 1870.

The Shakespeare – which was more like a tavern, situated on the corner with Virginia Street (then called Gorsey Lane) and the end of William Street – had only come into existence some seven years earlier to replace the old *Black Horse Inn*, Trap Lane (now Southbank Road).

The drunken brawl involved a John Barton who punched Richard Ackers to the ground, and who hit his head on the kerbstone and was picked up dead. Richard Ackers, who was a gardener in 1868, lived at 116 William Street (this part of the road is now Shakespeare Street). The house – along with No 114 – was a semi called Laurel Villas.

After the death of Richard Ackers, the house was taken over by an Elizabeth Ackers, who turned it into a lodging house. She disappeared around 1878 and the family name fails to appear in street directories at this time.

It is unclear who John Barton was as no details were given in the

The modern-day Shakespeare *pub – basically unchanged since the day of Barton and Ackers' fatal fight in 1870.* Author's collection

court reports – but we have a choice of a couple, recorded in street directories: a bath-chair proprietor from Hawes-Side is recorded in 1868 and 1870; as is a carter from Back Fleetwood Street (off Manchester Road) in 1868, who had moved to Hawes-Side by 1870, then Hall Street (1873 and 1876). However, a third John Barton is recorded in 1870, in Zetland Street, who could be the man listed in 1873 and 1876, as an oyster dealer in Southport's fish market. Take your pick.

Reported under 'Police Court' in the *Southport Visiter* on Friday,

Richard Acker's now tree-hidden house and front garden, originally in William Street. Sam Cookson

The entrance to the original police station, inside today's Town Hall. Author's collection

22 July 1870 – following a case of drunkenness including an assault on a policeman – this 'manslaughter case' had been heard the previous Tuesday, before the Mayor, J Glover; R Wild; W Halliwell, and R Craven, Esquires – all well-known and respected characters in Southport.

John Barton was brought up on remand, charged with having feloniously killed Richard Ackers, then an asphalter. Barton's brief, a Mr Barker, called his evidence for the prisoner's defence, in the shape of John Howard, a pipe layer from Scarisbrick, who said:

On Saturday night, about ten o'clock, I was at the front of the Shakespeare Hotel, *when I saw the prisoner, Ackers, and* [another man] *Rimmer come out. Ackers came out first and the other two came out together. Ackers walked on and then turned round and the prisoner came and stood up in front of him. I heard the prisoner say – 'Stand off.' I saw them holding up their fists and squaring up at each other and the prisoner struck the defendant about the face or chin. The latter fell over. The blow was not a heavy one. I cannot tell whether Ackers was drunk or sober. Afterwards the prisoner and the witness Rimmer began fighting. I went by the side of Ackers as he lay on the ground, and the prisoner stood by and remained there two or three minutes. I heard someone say that Ackers was killed, and the prisoner then went away, walking towards his home.*

Mr Barker's application for bail was accepted – the prisoner in £100 and two sureties at £50 each, and the Bench committed the prisoner for trial at the ensuing Liverpool Assizes.

When charged and cautioned by the Mayor, Barton said: 'It was an accident, and I am very sorry that it occurred. It was merely in self defence.' All we know after that is that at the Assizes, Barton was acquitted.

Chapter 2

The Suave Wife-Killing Doctor
The Promenade
1947

This was Southport's dramatic 'case of the century'. A nationally known episode of Dr Robert Clements who murdered his fourth wife, Mrs Amy Victoria Clements, then strongly suspected of poisoning his other three wealthy wives. When finally found out, he took the easy way out – poisoned himself.

Like most towns, Southport was just starting to recover from the hardships of war in 1947. Two of its largest hotels had been requisitioned by the War Ministry and a power crisis in February set the popular resort back a little. But, residents and businesses were looking forward to relieving summer visitors from their hard-earned holiday money. The town was proud of its genteel ambience, colourful gardens, tearooms, golden sandy beach, promenade and pier, and of course the sheltered and expensive shops on Lord Street.

Amongst the socialites spreading their wings was a sixty-six-year-old British physician and practicing 'bluebeard', the cunning Dr Robert George Clements. He was on his fourth wife, Amy, but was busy slowly killing her – after allegedly poisoning her three predecessors. The love of money may be the root of all evil and it is certainly a powerful motive for murder. In this case, it was murder by prescription.

Like most very big news stories the Clements case broke unexpectedly, in the quiet, Lancashire seaside resort one fine spring day; the discovery of a dying doctor – as mourners assembled for his wife's halted funeral – and then a second doctor committing suicide, obviously had immense possibilities. 'DEATH DRAMA OF DOCTOR AND WIFE' was the *Southport Visiter* headline on 31 May 1947.

The Clements case laid claim to be 'The Sensation of the Century,' the biggest story of its kind in twentieth century Southport, and could be labelled 'A Doctor's Diary of Death.' The startling story heralded world-wide publicity. The *Southport Visiter* told its readers, on Thursday, 26 June 1947:

TWO DOCTORS AND MRS CLEMENTS DIED FROM POISONING:

Morphine and Cyanide found in bodies.

Mr and Mrs Clements at a social function. Southport Visitor

At the time, Southport-residing Robert Clements was the only British doctor to be convicted of murder in the twentieth century (until Harold Shipman came along), and even then was never brought to trial in a court of law, but convicted by a coroner's jury. Like many other multiple murderers, he eventually became careless. Murdering his charming fourth wife in the same town as his third – in suspicious circumstances only eight years previously – was over-stretching the blarney. Multiple murderers are often remarkably arrogant, with a conceited belief they can hoodwink police, no matter how many clues they sprinkle; this is usually coupled with a desire to flaunt their expertise. Dr Clements fitted this category.

As he plotted the demise of each wife he paid court to and successfully wooed, the next Mrs Clements. His catch phrases included: 'whatever life throws at us', 'it can't go on' or 'there's nothing to be done', with his favourite being, 'it's just a matter of time'.

Doctors become poisoners in the same manner in which house-painters become artists – very rarely! However, a glance at any encyclopedia of murder would indicate that homicidal doctors take up an inordinate amount of space in the lists of the great poisoners. In his 1960 book *A Scientist Turns to Crime*, Dr James Brierley Firth said:

> *The Clements case remains one of the classic examples of murder by poison ... The gentle people of Southport were to be greatly shocked ... and the rest of the nation vastly intrigued.*

Although flamboyant and extrovert, Dr Robert Clements preferred to commit his crimes quietly, benefitting from a loophole in the law, namely, that it was perfectly legal for a British physician to treat his own wife if she was ill and to sign the death certificate without recourse to another doctor. It may have been unethical as far as the British Medical Association was concerned, but their rules were not the law of the land. It was not illegal, so ok by law, a fact Clements used to his full advantage.

Robert George Clements was born in Limerick in 1880 (some reports say 1882), and must have kissed the famous Blarney Castle stone, as he was certainly gifted with irresistible powers of persuasion. He had a certain power over women, and during his lifetime persuaded FOUR wealthy women to marry him – and to part with their not inconsiderable fortunes. He also used his blarney to coerce a young doctor to certify a false cause of death.

Robert – 'Bertie' to his friends – was a big bluff Irishman who studied in Edinburgh and at the age of twenty-four graduated in medicine in Belfast in 1904. He was already developing a paunch and pomposity. Attracted to Belfast's swinging social life, he liked to be seen in all the best restaurants, and attended theatres escorted by pretty women. But all this took money, more than a general practitioner could subscribe to, so the obvious solution was to marry someone with plenty of it and one who enjoyed socialising as much as he did.

Robert Clements was a very good doctor, some even said brilliant. A prominent figure in local medical circles, he held the Diploma of Public Health from Belfast, and became a Fellow of the Royal College of Surgeons in 1912, and a Fellow of the Faculty of Insurance (the year he took his FRCS examination). From time to time he also contributed to *The Lancet* and the *British Medical Journal*.

In 1912 (some say 1910) Bertie married for the first time, to Edyth Anna Mercier. Edyth (or Edith) was a somewhat plain woman, ten years his senior, but with the distinct advantage of having an immensely rich Belfast corn and grain merchant as a father. Not only did the wealthy miller give his socialite daughter a large sum of money as a wedding present, but he conveniently died eighteen months later leaving her another £25,000.

The couple were popular members of Belfast's society circle and lived well. They occupied a large detached house in one of the most prestigious suburbs and their wedding was one of the high spots on the social calendar. However, it soon became apparent that the dapper and debonair little doc was very much a ladies' man – he looked the part and acted the part. His marital record would later fully justify this observation. His philandering – and unsubtle flirtations – were certainly noted by many in the circles in which the Clements' moved.

Although Edyth was aware of his roving eye, she didn't seem to mind; at forty-two years of age she may have been flattered to have such a popular, suave husband, even if he did spend her money at a rapid rate. It took him just eight years to whittle away her fortune, coming to a head in 1920 when she was horrified to find her estate – or rather their joint account – had unaccountably dwindled to just £109. She remonstrated, but her financial worries were overshadowed by the onset of a somewhat unusual, yet serious ailment, which Clements diagnosed as a tropical 'sleeping sickness' disease, for which there was very little hope of a cure. It was thought she may have had advanced pancreas meningitis.

From the beginning it was 'only a matter of time'. Edyth died in the autumn of 1920, in Belfast, aged forty-five, with Clements signing the death certificate. After the funeral he sold his practice and moved to Manchester, became a GP, and engaged himself in similar sorts of social circles. He became a freemason, seen in all the best places, and of course, usually escorted by a pretty lady, particularly wealthy widows or daughters of well-to-do parents.

In 1921 Clements returned to Belfast to bring back a delicate and attractive daughter of a wealthy Manchester industrialist, who became his second wife during that summer, in Manchester. His 'lucky bride' was Ireland-born Mary McCleery (or MacCreary). She was another heiress gifted with a large sum of money on her marriage; so the doctor's good living pattern resumed. Although the second Mrs Clements was more critical of her husband's roving eye, their life-style was such that their funds were frittered away in four short years.

As the money dwindled, Mary was reported by her husband to be suffering from a heart complaint (rheumatic heart disease), and in 1925 – just four years after her marriage – she died suddenly. She was only twenty-five (some reports say twenty-seven) years old. Her husband furnished a death certificate saying she had succumbed to 'malignant endocarditis' (inflammation of the heart's lining). Clements confided to family friends: 'Mary's death had been expected.'

For the next two years Clements disappeared over the horizon becoming a ship's doctor, travelling extensively in the Orient. He returned in 1927, surprisingly, with a Japanese manservant, and set up practice back in Manchester. He soon reverted to his old ways, a medical Don Juan, becoming friendly with several wealthy women.

To the casual observer the paunchy, balding medic, would not have appeared to be a particularly attractive catch in the matrimonial stakes, so it must have been his social position and his rumoured wealth that attracted the ladies, for within a few years, he married again.

Bertie married for the third time in 1928, but on this occasion things did not run true to form. His choice was not a woman of substance but old family friend Sara Kathleen Burke, known as Kathleen (or Kathrine), who had known both his previous wives. This bonny, exuberant girl seemed to be the only one who was not wealthy – so perhaps the doc had found true love this time, as she survived over ten years. All the while, Dr Clements had been feathering his own nest, and with a successful practice was able to keep up his accustomed lifestyle, as long as he was reasonably frugal.

Around this time he became interested in 'fringe medicine' (alternative therapy) and experimented with hydrotherapy and herbalism, investigating the pros-and-cons of accepted Continental practices of giving most medicines by means of suppositories or anal douches.

In 1933, now fifty-three and semi-retired, he and Kathleen moved south and for two years ran a hotel at Bransgore, in the New Forest, but it was not a success. Kathleen's health was not at its best, so in 1935 they sold up, and moved to Kenworthy's Hydro, in 'sunny, healthy, Southport'. Here, the couple were as popular as ever. They renewed contact with many old Manchester friends, and appeared to be happy. But by 1938 Kathleen's small capital had almost expired, so Clements had to dig deep into his own pocket for a change.

Fond as Clements was of Kathleen, the situation was not what he had in mind, so from that time on his wife's life was in jeopardy. Surprise, surprise, she collapsed and died in late May 1939, at the fashionable Kenworthy Hydro, where Clements was now senior medical officer. On this occasion a local practitioner signed the death certificate, as 'tuberculosis' – which Clements had suggested, although some reports said it was stomach cancer.

For several weeks Clements had told friends of Kathleen's failing health, prophesying her imminent demise almost to the very day, when others thought she looked perfectly fit. The cremation certificate was signed by Clements and another local doctor, but for the third time there was no will, so the killer doctor again had to take out a grant of administration. She left just £489, a modest sum. Kathleen may not have had much money, but she did have friends. One of the closest happened to be a Southport lady doctor, Irene Gayus, who was not one to fall for Clements' charm, in fact, she disliked him intensely. Some people agreed with her, saying Dr Clements was a pompous, self-centred, power-mad 'quack'.

Dr Gayus was naturally upset at the death of her long-standing friend; she had always considered her to be lively and energetic, so was very surprised she had succumbed so quickly to cancer, especially after seeing her friend tuck away a hearty meal just two days before her death – something unlikely a person suffering stomach cancer could manage. Her suspicions had already been aroused during Kathleen's illness after friends in Manchester told her that Clements had signed the death certificate of his previous wife. Irene (known as 'Ireenie') was also aware that good old Bertie was openly having an affair with a very wealthy woman in the town, during the weeks prior to her good friend's death.

Dr Gayus's discoveries disturbed her deeply, so she sought out Southport's Chief Constable, Major Egan, to voice her fears and suspicions; he thought the matter serious enough to warrant action so events moved quickly.

Major Michael Joseph Egan, OBE, was a professional officer of considerable experience and ability, and well established with his quiet authority. He had set up the force's first traffic department (and police car) and pillar telephones, as well as the move to the present headquarters, from unsuitable premises below the Town Hall. He had been Southport's chief officer for nearly twenty years.

After consulting the coroner, Major Egan ordered a post-mortem. Unfortunately, by the time Sergeant WH Lloyd (who was promoted to Superintendent and Deputy Chief Constable in 1947) called the Liverpool mortuary to suspend the funeral – he was just fifteen minutes too late; Kathleen had already been cremated.

Whether or not Dr Clements was aware of Dr Gayus's misgivings is not known, but it seems highly probable that he knew nothing at all about the police intervention attempt, although if he had it might have saved two, if not three lives. Clements soon acquired his fourth wife, so wasn't a merry widower for long – and those fifteen minutes set a killer free, to strike again.

Twelve months on the fifty-seven year old was actively courting Amy Victoria Barnett, another Southport lady of means, nineteen years his junior, and in June 1940 Amy (or 'Vee' as she preferred to be called) had the doubtful distinction of becoming Mrs Clements IV. Her widowed father, one of Clements' few patients, was a Liverpool industrialist and managing director of the Liverpool Cartage Company (a shipping and banking tycoon), who had died unexpectedly, six months before the marriage, in January 1940. He left the heiress with a luxury flat on Southport's Promenade, and a hefty bank balance of £22,000, a considerable sum in those days. The imposing second-floor apartment at 20 The Promenade came in handy, as war was beginning in earnest, Kenworthy Hydro was requisitioned.

Wartime restrictions had scarcely had time to be felt when the wedding, in characteristic style, was held; it was an extremely opulent affair at St George's, Hanover Square, London, with a reception for several hundred guests at the *Mayfair Hotel*. The happy couple then returned to the luxurious Promenade flat, which had formerly been occupied by the bride's father. She was forty-seven years old, but not fated to reach forty-eight.

A wealthy man once more, Clements had no need to work, but in those first few months of 'the phoney war' he became a consultant/assistant medical officer at the Kenworthy Hydro, in Bath Street. The hydro was a health spa where well-to-do ladies with very minor ailments could receive major medical attention. As more doctors joined the Services, Clements was appointed Blackburn's Deputy Medical Officer of Health, commuting daily from Southport.

At home the couple appeared to be a most devoted pair, joining in many activities in the district. Vee was a talented pianist and musician and had several of her compositions published at her own expense. Both were keen on amateur theatricals, and were often seen at Southport Dramatic Society productions. He was also a member of the Southport Literary Society, the Film Society, and the Hospital Aid Society.

The doctor was a prominent freemason and active in the local Conservative party. The couple were pillars of the community during the war years, and his photograph regularly appeared in the *Southport Visiter* at one social function or another.

Mrs Clements didn't have her husband's brash, outgoing

personality, but busied herself doing good works around town, including serving on the International Women's Day Committee, and a staunch Christ Church worker, where her husband was a sidesman.

Social gadabouts they may have been, but they did little or no entertaining at their Promenade home. It was one of the best addresses in Southport, but few friends ever saw the inside of it. Clements used to boast that he had never eaten a cooked meal there, and let it be known that he and Vee preferred to eat out in cafes and restaurants – because Vee was such a poor housekeeper. He'd say that during their marriage she had hardly cooked a single meal at home. This seems to be borne out by the shocking state of their flat. This was not unusual for people of substantial means, so it attracted little comment, although their many acquaintances would have been horrified that they lived in such squalor in their fashionable abode, with evidence of neglect and decay all around them. The couple were, to say the least, a little peculiar in their ways.

The drama surrounding the almost inevitable death of the fourth Mrs Clements began in December 1946, when the top-rated physician and Chairman of Southport Infirmary Medical Board, Dr John Holmes, was called in by Dr Clements to examine his wife, who was suffering from violent headaches, giddiness and loss of memory. But Holmes could find nothing organically wrong with her, apart from 'symptoms of nervous illness'.

At this juncture, Dr Clements was not regarded as a very active medical practioner, being more or less retired, just keeping a select number of private patients. He had no proper plate on his door, no proper surgery, and no fixed hours, and for a while was not even on the telephone. But the couple were now quarrelling a great deal, and the flat was looking a real mess because she was a hoarder and 'didn't do house-cleaning work'.

In February 1947 she seemed to have improved and was out and about, but Dr Holmes heard that Clements was, surprisingly, telling friends that his wife was still very ill, again using his stock sinister prophecy, 'it was only a matter of time' (before she died). But this time it would be a case of fourth time unlucky.

One of these was his old friend Mrs Amy Winifred Stevens, a wealthy widow. He had telephoned her when his wife was ailing, asking if in the event of anything happening to his wife, could he go to her as a lodger, until he made other arrangements, which she agreed. He was obviously eye-ing up wife number five.

But then, on the eve of 26 May at midnight (Whit Monday), when she was in bed, Mrs Stevens was woken by loud knocking on her front door and someone shouting: 'Amy, come quickly, Vee is dying,' which was repeated several times. It was a sallow-looking Dr Clements, who had borrowed colleague Dr Andrew Brown's car, to tell her that his wife was seriously ill and asked if she would go round. Her son ran down while she dressed. The police were to obtain several details of Mrs Clements' last hours from Mrs Stevens. On reaching the flat, Mrs Stevens later stated:

When I arrived at the flat Mrs Clements was in bed. Her lips were swollen and very blue; her fingers were black to the second knuckle; her jaw had dropped; her face was inclined to be puffy; and her cheeks were of a pinkish tint.

Dr Brown lifted her eyelids, and said: 'The pupils are pin-point.' Dr Clements lifted the lids himself and said: 'Yes, yes.' I looked at Dr Brown and asked him what he would do if it was his wife, and he replied: 'Get her to the Infirmary or a nursing home.' Dr Clements, however, said he had promised Vee he would never put her into a home or hospital, but Dr Brown then said: 'Ring up Astley Bank Nursing Home,' which he did.

I went to the nursing home where Mrs Clements was put to bed. I stayed until Dr Brown came. A nurse came into the matron's room and said: 'It's not a cerebral haemorrhage.

While going home, I asked him [Dr Holmes] what he thought was wrong, and he said it was either hysteria through Mrs Clements' time of life, or a tumour on the brain.

Clements then rang Dr Holmes to say his wife was dying and asked him to find a nursing home as soon as possible, so he arranged for her to go to Astley Bank Nursing Home, 35 Scarisbrick New Road, where she was admitted in a comatose condition that night.

Dr Brown arrived and examined the unconscious Mrs Clements, along with the matron, Mrs Blodwen Baxendale and Dr Holmes.

Brown immediately noticed that Vee's eyes had pin-point pupils, and Mrs Baxendale said (which Dr Brown agreed): 'It looks more like morphine poisoning than cerebral trouble.'

Mrs Clements's skin was now a bluish tinge and she had difficulty breathing. All the symptoms pointed to morphine over-dosage. She remained unconscious throughout the night and died at 9.30 am the next day.

One side issue mentioned at the inquest was the fact that Dr Clements kissed Mrs Stevens 'goodbye' when she left. She said he had always done that, since they first met in 1937. Clements had apparently told her late husband that he would look out for her.

Dr John Holmes, a top-rated physician. Southport Visitor

Dr Clements, who had stayed overnight at the home, sleeping in a chair, was informed of his wife's demise and immediately talked

The former Astley Bank Nursing Home on Scarisbrick New Road. Cedric Greenwood

about cerebral tumour being the cause of death. But Dr Brown, a fairly new GP in Southport, was extremely doubtful of this, so conducted a post-mortem examination on her brain, which Clements agreed to. However, Dr Brown didn't tell the coroner or anyone else – which he was later severely criticized for – but had requested the assistance of Dr James Houston, a brilliant young pathologist at Southport Infirmary. Dr Houston also came from Northern Ireland and was a friend of the Clements's. He was an extremely conscientious man, indeed, something of a perfectionist. He found no evidence of a cerebral tumour, so decided to carry out a full post-mortem.

Dr Andrew Brown.
Southport Visiter

Dr Houston, primarily a haematologist, spent nearly four hours on the task; and, curiously, was conducted at the nursing home, a rather unsuitable location for such a procedure, especially as it became a full examination, not just an inspection on the brain.

After removing several organs Houston took blood samples, and went back to his laboratory for a detailed examination. Clements had hinted that his wife suffered from 'myeloid leukaemia' – an acute anaemia (malignant cancer) affecting the red corpuscles of the blood, turning them white. After the autopsy, Dr Houston asked his lab technician to incinerate the organs he had removed, despite not having examined any of them microscopically. Later that day he confirmed the existence of myeloid leukaemia, and signed the death certificate as such.

Houston, junior doctor though he was, must have been aware he should have sought consent of the coroner, Mr Bolton – and that disposing of specimens was out of order. They should have been returned to the body for burial or cremation.

Dr James Houston, the brilliant young pathologist at Southport Infirmary, who committed suicide.
Southport Visiter

218.	Twenty third May 1939 Kenworthys Hydro W.D.	Sarah Kathleen Clements	female	50 years	wife of Robert George Clements M.D.

a) myocarditis (b) malignant Pancreatitis Certified by E. A. Wilson M.B. 5-16	R. G. Clements Widower & deceased In attendance Kenworthys Hydro Bath Street Southport	Twenty fourth May 1939	H. Barr, Registrar

Death Certificate of Sarah Clements – with no mention of a morphine over-dose.
Author's collection

However, the suspicious Dr Brown, still far from happy, sought out the coroner, Mr Cornelius Bolton, who in turn informed Chief Constable, Lieutenant Colonel Harold Mighall. Southport Police had been 'interested' in Dr Clements for eight years – since the death of his third wife. A CID officer, Detective Miles, held a small file on the good doctor Clements, who had also been suspected of being an abortionist, but they didn't have any concrete proof. In light of these latest developments, they acted extremely quickly.

The police interviewed Clements' part-time charlady, a Mrs Keefe (another report calls her Miss Mary McKeefe, a servant in the next flat) who said Vee frequently lapsed into unconsciousness or had 'funny turns' that caused her to lose her voice; but her husband always seemed to know when these episodes were about to occur, and always told her not to come in the day before. She also said Vee's complexion gradually turned yellow over several weeks and she was incapable of doing any housework. The house was in a shocking condition, despite the efforts of Ms Keefe.

A devoted friend of Vee, Mrs Ursula Clarenden, told the police that Clements had barred her from the home for months to stop her having contact with his wife, because 'she needed rest', and later had the telephone removed so she couldn't even speak to her. Even so, Mrs Clarenden thought the whole affair was 'very disturbing'.

Police learned, from neighbours, that Clements seemed to have strange advance knowledge of his wife's 'dizzy spells'. During his wife's illness Dr Clements did not seem overcome with distress. Indeed he had been seen escorting a wealthy widow for most of the time another 'option' as wife number five.

But, most sinister of all, Clements had been writing prescriptions for enormous quantities of morphine sulphate tablets for various patients who never received the drug, strengthening the possibility that Mrs Clements had been deliberately turned into a morphine addict.

Lieutenant Colonel Harold Mighall, (later OBE) – the only Southport Chief to work his way through the ranks from Probationary Constable in 1925, aged twenty-four – had only been appointed in September the previous year. He took up the case personally, eager that this delicate situation was handled with care, although there wasn't much time. Amy's funeral was scheduled for Friday, 30 May, at Christ Church, which left very little time, so he quickly visited Dr Clements.

The doctor was strangely jovial for a man who had just lost his wife. He invited the senior policeman up to the flat who, to his surprise, found it to be filthy and smelling of rotting food. He thought the Clements' were wealthy enough to easily afford a maid to dispose of the empty milk bottles littering the floor, mixed with table scraps, half-eaten tins of food, newspapers and pill boxes. By a fireplace was a rotting grapefruit, along with a box of potatoes that had started to sprout; it was altogether a right mess. But that aside, Mighall wasn't there for small talk about house-cleaners, he said: 'I am interested in your wife's death,' he said bluntly. Clements appeared unperturbed.

'There is no cure for myeloid leukaemia. Dr Houston was quite correct in his findings,' Clements replied.

Mighall left it there, glad to get out into the fresh air. He then went to see Dr Houston, to ask if he was sure Mrs Clements died from natural causes. Houston became flushed and nervous:

I made a thorough examination and ascertained the cause of death. What could possibly be wrong with that?

The senior officer had been surprised that the nursing home's mortuary had not used, instead of the patient's bed. He then asked the young doctor: 'Can you tell me what you would think if you saw a patient with pin-point pupils?'

The doctor replied: 'That usually indicates morphine poisoning.'

Mighall was non-committal about there being a second post-mortem and left.

The new post-mortem on Vee was undertaken by a distinguished Home Office pathologist, Dr W H Grace. In the absence of most of the vital organs (which had been destroyed by Dr Houston) he was only able to certify that death was definitely not due to myeloid leukaemia.

Assisting him was the equally eminent Dr James Firth, Director of the Home Office's North Western Forensic, at Preston. With immense patience and consummate skill, Dr Firth continued the tests, and examined a minute portion of the kidney, a small amount of muscle, and a short section of spine weighing less than an ounce, where there appeared to be an injection mark. He conducted the difficult and exhaustive tests for over two weeks, but the remains resisted tests for virtually every known poison; finally, a microscopic section from the spinal cord responded to the presence of morphine. In a formidable feat of scientific deduction, Firth established, without doubt, that not only had Mrs Clements been poisoned slowly over a period of months, but that the fatal dose had been injected into the spinal region with a hypodermic needle, probably when the victim was unconscious.

When the young Dr Houston was told about the development and, after Dr Brown told him that he and Dr Holmes had strongly suspected Amy had been poisoned with morphine, Firth became extremely agitated, and replied: 'My God, I wish I had known about that earlier.'

Dr Firth's vital findings were passed to the police, and a warrant issued for Dr Clements' arrest. But, it was never implemented. Late in the evening before Amy's funeral ceremony, a funeral director representative called at the Clements' home to make final arrangements, but discovered the doctor in bed, unconscious. Unable to rouse him he called the police, and in the early hours of Friday, 30 May – the day of the funeral – Inspector Hoyle and PC

Harry Holland hurried to Dr Clements' Promenade apartment.

The noose was hovering around Dr Clements's neck – but he escaped the full pain of justice. Realising his fate, he had taken a massive dose of morphine and the officers found him unconscious in his kitchen. He was taken to Southport Infirmary, but died a few minutes after admission, due to the self-inflicted drug injection.

He had left an envelope addressed to 'Ernest and George' (his only son and brother-in-law). Inside was a defiant and audacious suicide note, in which he denied his crime to the last; it simply read:

To whom it may concern – I can no longer tolerate this diabolical insult to which I have recently been exposed.

The Chief Constable continued with his plan and ordered Amy Clements' funeral service to be stopped and the body removed for a second post-mortem. But mourners had already gathered at Southport's oldest church, so were shocked and surprised when policemen arrived to call it off until further notice. Scandalising whispers were exchanged as the puzzled mourners stood in groups, asking why the funeral of a respected medical man's wife be halted in such fashion. The *Southport Visiter*'s front page headline screamed:

DRAMA OF DOCTOR AND WIFE – FUNERAL STOPPED AS MOURNERS ASSEMBLED

Dr Firth helped to examine Clements's flat with the police, finding it in a state of indescribable confusion and filth. Rancid groceries were stacked high in the kitchen, bedclothes consisted of black, dirty blankets, coal was piled everywhere, even under the kitchen table.

But more significant was the discovery of dozens of bottles of tablets in almost every room; some were empty, others were labelled 'phenobarbitone' – but were actually grains of morphine sulphate tablets. One bottle was found on the mantelpiece in the bedroom, with the prescription mark, 'The Tablets – one night, one morning.' However, this also did not contain material corresponding to the prescription, but small morphine tablets. Other material recovered from Clements' flat included a glass phial (syringe), containing the crystallised deposit of a marked amount of morphine. It was obvious that Mrs Clements had been given these tablets over a very long period – she had slowly been poisoned.

Dr Robert Clements was to be declared a murderer only on the verdict of a coroner's jury. That he avoided the risk of a criminal trial and long sentence, if only for the murder of his fourth wife, by killing himself, implies an admission of guilt. But the public didn't know these details until the coroner's inquest was over; and no-one knew it would turn out to be 'The Case of the Century.'

Southport was its usual peaceful self on that late spring morning in May as local newspaper reporters assembled for 'routine' inquests at Southport's Magistrates' Court – until there was a whispered 'tip-off' and within hours the resort was over-run with press-hounds from all corners of the land. They started a train of enquiries that culminated in one of the most sensational inquest stories of all time. Their very own 'inquest' was about to take place in that very court.

A trickle of brief messages began to flash from the Albert Road courtroom to newspaper offices and press agencies around the country – 'Dr Clements found dying in flat as wife's funeral is stopped by Coroner' – gave the principal character worldwide notoriety.

Before the day was through the converging hacks had picked up many threads regarding the private life of Dr Clements; their stories found a place in newspapers all over the UK as well as overseas. For three full days there was no peace for the Southport journalists, the much harassed police officials and, residents who had known Dr Clements or any of his four wives.

The mystery of Mrs Clements's death, followed so dramatically by her husband's suicide, had caused a major sensation, but after a few days, it seemed that interest in the story was beginning to wane. Newspaper men left the town in increasing numbers until news of a second sensation brought them scurrying back.

There was one more catastrophe to come.

On 2 June, the thirty-nine-year-old pathologist, Dr James Montague Houston, who had performed the post-mortem on Mrs Clements – strangely on the insistence of Dr Clements – was found dead in his laboratory at Southport Infirmary. He was found slumped in an

The jurors in the famous Dr Clements murder case. Southport Visiter

armchair, with the unmistakable odour of bitter almonds, indicating cyanide. He had indeed committed suicide by taking an exceptional amount of a highly-concentrated solution of sodium cyanide. It was in fact 300 times more than required for a fatal dose. So, it was a double suicide situation. Dr Houston, appalled by his precipitate and inaccurate diagnosis, left a more plaintive message:

I have for some time been aware that I have been making mistakes. I have not profited by my experience. I was convinced that Mrs Clements died of leukaemia, and accordingly destroyed the vital organs after completing my autopsy.

The headline on page one of the *Southport Visiter*, Tuesday, 3 June, read:

DRAMATIC NEW TURN IN SOUTHPORT MYSTERY
POST MORTEM ON INFIRMARY PATHOLOGIST

For many people the most tragic part of this extraordinary affair was the death of this rather quiet, shy and reserved young doctor. It was a terrible tragedy that a man like him should have lost his life because of an innocent connection with this curious case. A diabetic who needed to take insulin, Dr Houston was a brilliant pathologist and popular with his colleagues. Dr Grace later said:

> *He was more the research type. I think he was more fitted for that sort of work, than the very trying and worrying work in the pathological department of a hospital.*

Dr Houston had started work as a pathologist at the Infirmary just five months earlier at a salary of £1,250 a year. Throughout the war he had served at Catterick Camp as pathologist, with the rank of Major, and became the senior surgeon responsible for 8,000 troops. He was happily married with two young sons, and only two weeks earlier had moved into a house of their own, after a spell in

Umbrella sharing crowd outside the court. Southport Visiter

rather cramped lodgings. His wife said he had been suffering the strain of overwork for some time. Just before she sailed for Ireland to attend her husband's funeral, Mrs Houston handed a note to a journalist saying:

For the Press. My life belonged to my husband – therefore there is nothing more to be said.

Dr Edward Cronin Lowe, Southport Infirmary's honorary consultant pathologist, said:

My opinion is that Dr Houston's diagnosis was an honest and genuine one, but based on insufficient evidence. In some inexplicable way his usually careful mental approach to a problem had been biased. He only had to revise his previous diagnoses, but unfortunately, being of a reserved and reticent nature, did not confide in those who would have gladly helped him, and took this most regrettable step which closed a highly specialised and brilliant professional career.

The ongoing double inquest had suddenly become a more interesting triple one.

On Tuesday, 25 June, the coroner's (triple) inquest on Mrs Clements, Dr Clements and now Dr Houston was opened by the Southport coroner, Mr Cornelius Bolton. The courtroom was thronged by sightseers.

Many of the reporters who had returned to the town following the second suicide, did not leave until after this triple inquest, which was the longest in local history, extending over four days; more than sixty newspaper representatives attended. The most difficult aspect of the case was undoubtedly to give a factual report of the happenings and history of Dr Clements and not to allow a too vivid imagination to turn a sensational story into a fantastic one. Where imagination was allowed free play the words of Mr Cornelius Bolton, the coroner at the inquest, are self-explanatory. He said:

Within each hours of each death, press detectives commenced their investigations. Having ferreted out the matter many laid their own construction of events and did almost everything except return verdicts.

Chequebook journalism is certainly nothing new, and criticism of the press treatment of the case was expressed by Mr W Bentley, President of the Coroners' Society of England and Wales. Mr Bentley referred to reporters who:

Visited Southport by aeroplanes, their pockets stuffed with money, prepared to buy any information they could get. If anyone reads anything that looks as if it might have come from the Coroner, you may tell anyone you may discuss it with that it is a lie. It is the imagination of other people, certainly not the information of the Coroner.

The coroner also expressed similar criticism of newspapers sending snooping wallet-bulging reporters; he warned the jury, and the public for that matter, that any reports purporting to reflect either his opinion or the opinions of the police, should be totally disregarded until the inquest was over and the verdicts returned. I don't suppose any of the sub-editors would have been flippant enough to use a Cluedo phrase: Dr Clements; on the Promenade; in the bedroom; with poison!

Dramatic evidence that Mrs Amy Victoria Clements and her husband Dr Robert George Clements, both died from morphine poisoning while Dr Houston died from cyanide poisoning, was given by Dr W H Grace, the Home Office Pathologist.

There had been a great deal of discrepancy over Dr Clements' account of his wife's illness and evidence brought by various friends of Vee. Clements had constantly referred to his wife's increasing disorientation and lassitude, though friends claimed the couple were seen regularly dining out in Lord Street restaurant and cafes, and that she seemed perfectly normal.

The police produced their evidence, including statements from more than fifty people, chiefly in and around Southport, but other inquiries had taken them to Liverpool, Blackburn and other towns in West Lancashire, but the police denied that any Ulster CID had been involved in the case. However, the most dramatic moment came when Detective Sergeant J H Thompson produced an odd feature for police evidence – the contents of Dr Clements' diary.

This carefully-kept document contained almost daily, descriptive details, revealing the slow decline of his wife's health. On 26 May

1947, when Mrs Clements was taken to the nursing home, where she died, Dr. Clements, appearing to be grief stricken, wrote:

Adorable wife, she was good and devoted, never fair to herself.

The diary evidence centred on abnormalities in some of the statements. One interesting passage was the death of his wife having taken place fifteen minutes before it actually did; and even stranger, according to a family friend, he had telephoned them at five minutes to nine that morning, telling them she was already dead. Another statement covered the evening immediately prior to his wife's death. He wrote:

Set out for a walk in the afternoon. Tea at home. After tea went for a walk to the Post Office. Vee commenced to lose voice and the power of her limbs. Got her home with difficulty and with a fearful headache. Got her to bed. Prepared tea. Felt better for it. After washing-up found her unconscious. Sent for Dr Brown; later Dr Holmes.

Dr Clements had also said that at one point she collapsed on the Promenade. And yet, according to the evidence of lynx-eyed neighbour, Mrs Jean MacLachlan, the Clements' had gone for a walk, but had returned arm-in-arm at 10.15 pm, laughing and joking and seemingly in good health and spirits on the doorstep while the doctor fumbled for his key. The last diary entry was 29 May, when he had officially identified his wife's body, stating:

Police rang up and came and brought me to identify Vee at the morgue for inquest tomorrow morning. What is it all about?

When the hearing was resumed (on the Tuesday), Mrs Amy Winifred Stevens continued her evidence, telling the coroner that she and her husband had been friendly with Dr and Mrs Clements since about 1937, and that they both had always seemed very happy. She described how Mrs Clements appeared to her in the October, saying she was very amazed when she looked at her face, which appeared to 'have gone very small and very white'.

Dr Clements' wealthy friend, Mrs Amy Winifred Stevens.
Southport Visiter

Just before Christmas Clements told Mrs Stevens that his wife was still very poorly, and he gave her the same reply when she saw him on a later occasion, adding that other doctors had told him it was 'only a matter of time'. *Southport Visiter* readers were riveted to the details of the Clements case, and the reporters gave them full coverage. On Saturday, 7 June 1947, the page one lead was:

Clements case nears completion

In his summary, the coroner said to the jury:

Does it not seem strange that a woman with no obvious organic disease should apparently be well at 10.15 pm but that she should be unconscious and dying within the next hour?

The coroner also pointed out that the apparent lack of motive for Clements to kill his wife was immaterial. If they thought it was a wilful act on his part they should return a verdict accordingly. As regards the death of Dr Clements himself, the coroner wished to be as fair as possible to a man who was no longer present and in no position to defend himself or explain his actions. His death was either *felo de se*, self-murder, or suicide while of unsound mind.

In the case of Dr Houston similar conditions prevailed, except that it was known he had a history of depression, the coroner considered that Dr Houston took his own life whilst his mind was disturbed.

The coroner took the opportunity of thanking the police for their rapid action in investigating the death of Mrs Clements, and in particular, Dr Firth, who performed a difficult task with such sparse material.

The coroner's jury brought in a verdict of 'Murder' *felo de se* in respect of Clements.

One of the members of the jury was the well-known John (Jack) Clough, proprietor of the *Bold Hotel*, Lord Street, a local councillor and vice-chairman of Southport Football Club. The others were: Major J M Greer (foreman); Miss Helen Sumner; Miss Evelyn Wynne; John Bailes; William Rickerby; George Chandler; Eric Donevein, and Percy Woods.

The inquest jury returned the following verdicts:

Mrs Clements was murdered by Dr Clements.

Dr Clements committed felo de se.
Dr Houston took his life while the balance of his mind was disturbed.

The smartest bit of reporting came at the end of the inquest. Prior to the verdicts being returned, the court doors were locked to prevent a rush by journalists eager to get the news away. In fact, the verdicts were known in Fleet Street before the doors were unlocked and before the people waiting in the court corridor knew. Without the use of the modern mobile phone, one enterprising reporter pushed a slip of paper underneath a door to a colleague waiting outside and a few seconds later he was telephoning the information to London.

Local residents disregarded the inclement weather to queue up outside the Law Courts to hear the latest news, live, as the drama unfolded.

As the main culprit was now dead the police took no further action regarding the deaths of the three previous wives, which, in any case, had taken place so long before.

There was now no point in delaying Amy's funeral any longer, and it was allowed to take place at Birkdale Cemetery, Duke Street, on 31 May. The *Southport Visiter* noted a considerable amount of wreaths, including those from Southport Zionist and Literary Society, Vicar and Mrs Pickering, of Christ Church, the Society and Friends of Czechoslovakia, and one, simply marked 'husband'.

But, there was still the case of motive. Clements undoubtedly killed his first two wives when their money ran out, and possibly the third when his own finances became strained. But with Vee money did not appear to be the motive.

Two wills made by Dr Clements were found, dated February and March 1944, leaving his estate of £12,000 to his son. Mrs Amy Clements appeared to follow the example of her husband's first three wives by not making a will, despite having an estate estimated at over £50,000 gross. In view of the coroner's verdict Clements could derive no benefit from his wife's estate, which passed in due course to her near relatives. Two unofficial handwritten draft wills for both the Clements' were discovered, dated May 1942, which gave the same information. So, with regard to his fourth wife, was it a marriage for love or money?

Out of the SIX deaths connected with Dr Clements, four took

place in the town and at least one (Dr Houston) could have been prevented. However, some people in Southport didn't seem to worry too much about that, as the Southport Visiter (3 June 1947) disclosed:

> *For the past two days house-hunters have been arriving at 20 The Promenade, all wanting to take possession of the flat formerly occupied by the unfortunate Mrs Amy Clements and her murdering husband, Doctor Robert George Clements.*

Dr Clements was interred at Birkdale Cemetery on Tuesday, 3 June. There were few mourners apart from the dead man's close relatives and only one wreath, a five-foot cross of roses, inscribed 'From George and Ernest'. No headstone marks his grave today.

Despite the inconsistencies in his diary, plenty of people said Vee appeared to be well and happy throughout her marriage to the doctor. But perhaps he tired of her and saw his wife as a barrier to further amorous conquests.

Dr Clements was most certainly a wily bird, but in the end a careless one. He does not seem to have studied sufficiently the subject of murder by morphine. Had he done so, he could have instilled atropine into his wife's eyes which would have dilated the pupils, masking the characteristic pin-points which denote the presence of morphine.

On 3 July 1947, in the House of Commons, Stockport's MP asked:

> *In view of a recent case at Southport, was the Minister of Health aware that the law permitted medical practitioners to issue death certificates in respect of close relatives, and if he proposed legislation to end this practice?*

The Minister, Mr Aneurin Bevan, replied that he was not contemplating any change in the law. Britain, at that time, remained almost the only country in the civilized world where a doctor could issue a death certificate in respect of his own family.

The whole murderous episode has come down through the years and on Tuesday, 18 January 1994, a half-hour episode of Granada TV's true crime series *In Suspicious Circumstances* was broadcast, presented by Edward 'The Equaliser' Woodward, entitled *The Next*

The architecturally splendid Normanhurst, 15 Lord Street West, once the home to wife-murdering Dr Robert Clements. Cedric Greenwood

Mrs Clements. This dramatized mystery provided an intriguing look at Dr Clements (portrayed by Dudley Sutton), a respected doctor who loved too many women in pre-World War Two Southport, and how a veil of mystery still lingers, because the money-mad medic was never actually brought to trial.

Historically, Dr Clements' abode at 15 Lord Street West, Normanhurst, was built in 1839, and was the last of the early 'marine villas' built in an area known as 'Over the (river) Nile' – later Nile Square – before Birkdale Park was laid out in 1850. In his 1971 book *Thatch, Towers & Colonnades* architectural historian Cedric Greenwood said:

> *This house has a façade which is quite unique in Southport, in an*

Kenworthy's Hydropathic Hotel, *Bath Street.* Author's collection

indefinable free style of architecture. It is a symmetrical composition of semicircular arches, balustrading, corbels and terra-cotta decoration with steeped gables capped by semicircular pediments.

Formerly a private residence, it was a hotel from 1925 to 1960, when it was divided into luxury apartments. The house was originally part of a secluded square, partitioned by the resort's first house, the *South Port Hotel* (Duke's Folly), and became – which is hard to imagine – part of the busy A565 main road axis, along which the linear borough of Southport is built. The original dated boundary stone separating Southport from Birkdale still survives on the wall in the front garden.

Another residency was at Kenworthy Hydro. Early in the twentieth century Southport had four large hydropathic establishments, offering a wide range of water-based treatments.

Named after the physicians Arthur and Irene, Kenworthy's, in Bath Street, was one of them, opening in 1877. It was still going in the 1930s but had become a hotel (certainly by 1936), and subsequently became private residences. The frontage is virtually unchanged to this day.

The Clements' Promenade address was next door to the *Waverley's Hotel*. Built about 1888, as a thirty-six bedroomed commercial temperance hotel, it was later extended by taking over No 20, the doctors' house. This then became the *Bailey's Hotel* which ran alongside Scarisbrick Avenue. The *New Bailey's* was advertised in 1992 as the former home of 'one of Britain's most infamous murders – whose ghost still abounded'.

The home that Mrs Amy Clements died in, Astley Nursing Home, at 35 Scarisbrick New Road, is another fine architectural piece. Cedric Greenwood also featured this property in his book, calling it one of the most handsome examples of Victorian

The doctor's stylish address, the Waverley Hotel, *on the Promenade.* Author's collection

domestic architecture in the town. It was built about 1880 as Dudley House, the home of the then Deputy Clerk of the Peace for Lancashire, Samuel Campbell Hulton Sadler. Re-named Hollinwood in more recent times, it is built in glazed red Accrington brick and yellow sandstone. Its beautiful features are the stone bow windows, arcaded balustrading over the square bay windows, curved gables and the porch. It can also boast a beautiful stained glass window which floods the stairway with coloured light. It's such a shame it has been neglected for many years, to become a sorry-looking, run-down house separated into flats.

Police officers on the Dr Clements case. Southport Visiter

Chapter 3

Who Killed Draper Harry?
Bootle
1958

*The baffling murder of respected businessman, Harry Baker,
who was found stuffed in two coal sacks in a field. He had
been abducted in broad daylight, robbed of just £25,
and battered to death, sustaining a fractured skull.
Some fifty years later the incident is still unsolved.*

Over 100 unsolved murders – some dating back to the turn of the last century – lie in the dusty archives of Merseyside Police's Headquarters. Every now and then they are taken down from the shelf and dusted off – especially when new technology may help solve the crime.

The Harry Baker murder is one such case that will never be closed.

During a private, tense, police conference in a Liverpool police station on Tuesday, 24 June 1958, senior detectives from Liverpool and Cheshire were told they were facing a baffling crime. The body of a well-respected Southport man, who had been quickly identified as being Harry Baker, had been found on 23 June, stuffed in two coal sacks in a field on the A50, the Llandudno road, at High Legh, near Knutsford. He had been battered to death and robbed.

Murder victim, Harry Baker, of Melling Road. Daily Post

Jesse Wood, of Warrington, who discovered Mr Baker's body. Daily Post

During the conference a Detective Chief Superintendent informed the other detectives that Mr Baker's body appeared to have been taken a long way before being dumped at the roadside. The body was found by a roadman, Jesse Wood, of Warrington, who had detected a 'funny smell' while cutting grass at the roadside nearby, and gone to investigate.

The woman's nylon stocking used to strangle him was still wound round his neck. Although Harry's murderer would have been covered in blood, little did they know that nearly fifty years later this murder case would still be unsolved.

The sixty-one year old credit draper, from Melling Road, had sustained severe head injuries, including a fractured skull, and had obviously been beaten to death with a blunt instrument. His jacket had been removed and the only thing left in his pockets was a return train ticket from Southport to Bankhall. Just £25 in cash, a fountain pen and two watches were taken.

Detectives rushed to Dudley, Worcestershire, after a report that a suspicious looking man had taken a wristwatch, resembling one

Melling Road, just off Roe Lane. Sam Cookson

Looking for clues where Mr Baker's body was discovered. Daily Post

that had belonged to Mr Baker, into a jeweller's, but this gained no positive lead in their investigation. Apparently, the man took the watch into the shop for repair, but took it away again after being told how much it would cost.

Detective Chief Superintendent Fred Turner, head of Cheshire County CID, who led the murder hunt, interviewed the jeweller and took a statement from him. A widespread search for this watch and also a gold wristwatch carried by Mr Baker, both presumably taken by the killer, yielded no results.

Although few murders went unsolved in the 1950s, the detectives knew this was going to be an uphill task, despite finding it easy to trace Mr Baker's known clients, through what turned out to be his meticulous business records.

Bludgeoned, choked and robbed, then dumped in a field near Warrington, covered by more sacks, the murderous act on Harry Baker instantly grabbed the attention of the public. Newspaper headlines revealed that a brutal murder had been discovered and that some fiend was still stalking the North West's streets.

The inquest on Harry Baker opened on 23 June, and resumed a little later, in July. A post-mortem examination disclosed that death was due to head injuries and asphyxia.

Bootle police headquarters in Oriel Road became the centre of police inquiries, with detectives checking and re-checking hundreds of statements and other items of information. They were convinced that somewhere in the square mile area centred on Strand Road, Bootle, where Mr Baker was last seen alive, was someone who could supply a vital clue to the identity of the murderers. They appealed to the public for information to establish the definite pattern of Baker's last movements between 1pm and 3pm on 6 June, the day he vanished.

Meanwhile, rumours rapidly circulated through the teeming streets around Liverpool's docks. Children were told that Baker had been found with his eyes poked out so no one could look into them and see the face of his killer.

It later emerged that after a business trip to Liverpool, Harry had been missing for seventeen days, and was then kidnapped (or abducted) in broad daylight, so little was known of his movements. Detectives discovered that he should have called at a house at 1.10pm on 7 June, but he never showed up.

He was last seen at 1.45 pm talking to a smart, thin-faced man at a bus stop outside the *Derby Arms* on Strand Road, in Bootle. They discovered he often took the bus into Liverpool for lunch when he was in the city. But it begs the question, if he was waiting at the bus stop why did he break with his regimented routine and miss visiting a client?

Strand Road, Bootle, in 1958, where Southport resident Harry Baker was last seen.
Daily Post

The nylon stocking found tied round his neck suggested a female accomplice and detectives realised it would have taken more than one person to bundle Mr Baker's body into the back of a van or car, before throwing it over a fence into a field.

Detectives also believed that the ladies' stocking suggested Harry met his death in a house, probably in one of the thousands of terraced houses where Harry did his business.

The thin-faced man also re-emerged in later enquiries. A garage owner remembered seeing a driver fitting his description on the evening of Mr Baker's disappearance. He told the police:

He was dirty and excited and had a black or dark green van with a twisted bumper. He asked the way to Knutsford.

Other drivers remembered seeing a van parked at the spot where Mr Baker's body was found the day after he went missing.

Theories abounded about the cause of death. Had a robber used insider knowledge of his meticulous routine to entice Mr Baker, which led to his death?

More than 30,000 people were interviewed and a reward of £500 was offered for the capture of the killer. Interpol and the Garda in Ireland were contacted, but no clue was ever found.

It would seem that any murder inquiry attracts random confessions, prank clues and hoax witnesses, but detectives investigating the Harry Baker murder must have felt they were faced with another prankster when, in 1964 – six years after the murder – they were sent an astonishing letter.

The baffling note, sent by an anonymous elderly lady from Wallasey, to Chief Inspector William Cotter, was rambling and incoherent in parts, but told a gruesome and disturbing tale. It begins unpromisingly, when the woman says:

You must bear in mind I am a deserted wife and therefore prone to malice, so you must accept this as you see fit.

She then goes on to describe a dream she had in which she saw her husband standing beside the body of Harry Baker. She continues in her letter:

To those in charge of the case it is a mystery as to why and who was responsible for the death of Harry Baker, but not to me, a complete stranger to the man. Why did I dream the scene before it even hit the headlines? I remember the dream so well, it was so vivid and real and yet I gave it no further thought, until I saw the Daily Post headlines and was so scared.

She dreamt she was in the countryside when she suddenly came across a body concealed in some sacks. Her estranged husband and his lover were standing over the body sneering at her. After waking up she saw the news headlines and in tears told her mother what she had just dreamt. But it was six years before she could bring herself to go to the police.

Was her husband the killer?

The trail was cold and the police were unable to link him with the killing. They never discovered what finally prompted the woman to write to the police after so long. The woman herself did not contact them again and her letter finished eerily:

Only the killer could have seen what I saw. Perhaps time will catch up with him, perhaps not, but I will always wonder why I dreamed what I did.

In 1981, Edward Moore, from Huyton, Liverpool, was questioned about the Baker murder – after completing a twenty-one-year jail sentence for murder in Morocco – but was released without charge.

The murder case has remained open ever since.

Chapter 4

Little Girl Under a Porter's Bed
Palace Hotel
1961

The chilling murder of a little six-year-old girl, Amanda Graham,
who was abducted as she made her way home from the fairground,
and sexually attacked then strangled by Alan Wills,
a porter at the impressive Grand Palace Hotel, *Birkdale,*
who dumped Mandy under his bed.

The ever-present threat to young children out playing, walking or travelling unsupervised, is not just a sign of modern times. This is a forty-five year old chilling warning to all parents. It is the disturbing murder of a six-year-old girl who was abducted as she made her way home from the resort's fairground, then sexually attacked, strangled, and dumped under the bed of a child murderer – a porter at Birkdale's *Palace Hotel*.

The incident, of course, horrified the town's folk.

The debate on re-introducing the death penalty is an on-going one. Even those who support its abolition would consider bringing it back for child killers. However, despite newspaper campaigns and calls by the media each time a child is brutally murdered, under the Homicide Act of 1957, child murders were deemed no longer worthy of the death penalty. If it wasn't for this Act, the brutal killer of a young Southport girl would be lying in a felon's

Little Amanda Graham, of Hartwood Road, who was brutally murdered at the Palace Hotel. Author's collection

grave, rather than being one of the longest prisoners currently held in captivity.

The magnificent Birkdale *Palace Hotel* was one of Southport's best-known and popular Victorian structures, in the days when Birkdale was a separate borough. Although dominating the seafront, it was something of a white elephant, as its location was never quite satisfactory. After opening in November 1866, it failed to take off and was re-launched as a hydro hotel in 1881, offering water-based health treatment – to compete with the big inland spa town resorts for the wealthy long-stay convalescence and chronically-ill market.

The hotel was taken over by the American Red Cross in 1942 and used as a rest home for the US Army until 1945, becoming one of the largest rehabilitation centres in the country. The going was tough after that, especially in the 1950s when the prestigious hotel ran out of cash; its final owners went into liquidation and the business was wound up in 1967.

Long gone are the days when legend had the hotel being haunted by the dead architect who allegedly committed suicide because the hotel had been built the wrong way round, or back-to-front. This,

The impressive Birkdale Palace Hotel, *the scene of one of Southport's most heartbreaking murders.* Author's collection

in fact, is not true, as all three architects lived long and happy lives – but try telling that to the workmen who 'witnessed' the spooky events whilst taking the elegant structure apart.

The *Palace Hotel* was demolished early in 1969 amid huge local publicity. Partly because of the hotel's prestige, but the other reason for such public interest was the hotel's notoriety for more mysterious and sinister reasons. Local legend (falsely) claims that the architect committed suicide after discovering the hotel had been built 'back-to-front', with its grandiose façade facing inland instead of seaward. Other stories tell of two sisters dying in a suicide pact at the hotel.

However, the most grisly was the murder of little Amanda Graham.

The hotel never really recovered from being tainted by this horrific child murder. As a result its premier reputation was irreparably damaged and the hotel lost its way, staggering on for just six more years. But still, the decision to demolish it came as a great shock to residents, and the council had expected it to be re-opened. The site is now packed with bungalows and dormers nestling around a gently curving crescent forming Ascot Court estate.

It all began on a warm sunny evening on Wednesday, 23 May, during the summer of 1961, about 5.15 pm, when three young girl friends went to enjoy themselves at the resort's amusement park – Pleasureland.

Closed and dismantled between 2006-07, the fairground's attractions available to a young child at this time included, amongst many others; the 1001 Mirrors, Children's Roller-Coaster, River Caves, Dodgems, Ghost Train, The Skidding Swirl (later called The Black Hole), the Funhouse, and maybe the Hurricane Jets; and not forgetting the candy-floss and ice-cream.

One of the girls was six-year-old Amanda Graham – known as 'Mandy' – a friendly and talkative child. Mandy, who had shoulder-length dark-hair, was the youngest daughter of forty-seven-year-old Terence Graham, a sheet-metal worker, and his thirty-eight-year-old wife, Veronica. The couple had two older children, twenty-year-old Michael, a chef at a Lord Street restaurant, and seventeen-year-old Pauline, who had just started to work at a holiday camp. The

Pleasureland and Peter Pan's were the venues for Amanda Graham's last moments as a little girl. Stephen Copnall

Holy Trinity School, off Manchester Road. Sam Cookson

family also had a seafood stall at Southport Indoor Market (and one at Wigan market), which was managed by Mrs Graham.

Still wearing her Holy Trinity school blazer, she asked her mother if she could go the fairground with her friends, Freda and Linda. Both these girls were much older than Mandy, so her mum, Veronica, agreed, and watched as she skipped happily away from their market stall. That was the last time her mother saw her young daughter.

As darkness fell the tender aged girl had still not returned home, her worried parents telephoned the police, but their missing person's enquiry took a sinister twist when several police witnesses reported Mandy being seen on a number of occasions, in the company of a man. One witness said she saw Mandy holding the man's hand strolling down the Promenade, while another saw her having a shoulder-ride, heading for Manchester Road.

Mandy was last seen getting off a Corporation bus, unescorted, shortly before 7.40 pm, close to her home at 26 Hartwood Road – but she never arrived there, she disappeared on that summer night. She had been abducted. At 9.15 pm (some reports say 10.15 pm) her anxious parents telephoned the police to report her as missing, and intensive inquiries began. No 26 Hartwood Road, a detached house, was previously the home of a well known vicar, the Reverend W Field, who died on 8 January 1924.

No 26 Hartwood Road, home to the Graham family. Sam Cookson

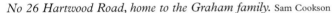

Southport Police at the Palace Hotel *murder scene.* Daily Post

Police tracker dogs were quickly drafted in and other police forces assisted, and very soon a name for the mystery man was established. He was identified as thirty-three-year-old Alan Victor Wills, a kitchen and hotel porter employed at the *Palace Hotel*. Officers found Wills' staff room locked, and were informed that he wasn't on duty, and couldn't be found, so they left to pursue their enquiries elsewhere.

Enquiries that night proved fruitless so descriptions of Wills and Mandy were posted to seaport and airline staff, as well as railway and bus stations. Wills, who was originally from Royton, Oldham, was described as five foot three inches tall, with dark brown hair and a hooked nose. He also had a withered right hand which made his arm noticeably shorter than the other, and his arms and hands were heavily tattooed. Little Amanda, who had big dark eyes, was described as having bobbed brown hair, and last seen wearing her school blazer.

Numerous hotels and boarding houses were visited by the police, but no-one of their description had been seen. Southport detectives contacted their colleagues in Oldham to look out for the pair, as were those in Chesterfield, as Wills was known to have friends there.

Unaware that he was a marked man, Alan Wills reported for kitchen duty at 9.25 am the next day (Thursday), but after being told the police were looking for him he made a lame excuse to go to his room – and then he disappeared. Tipped off that Wills had been seen, Detective Sergeant Mackenzie Folan and uniformed officers raced back to the *Palace Hotel*, and at 10.45 am knocked on the door of staff bedroom No 13. With no reply, DS Folan forced the flimsy locked door open with his shoulder, and unfortunately, abandoned underneath the bed, draped with a man's clothing, was the dead body of little Amanda Graham. The poor youngster, who was still bound-up and practically naked, had been sexually violated.

The missing person's case had become a nationwide murder hunt, and heading the search was Chief Constable Joe Pessell, who assigned every available policeman on the case.

Medical evidence was called at 'an appropriate time' to show that the child had been criminally and sexually assaulted and suffocated. Dr Charles St-Hill, the Home Office pathologist, carried out a post-mortem and confirmed that asphyxiation (suffocation), due to pressure on the throat and neck, was the cause of death, and that prior to death she had been raped. Amanda's father went to the *Palace Hotel* about 12 noon to identify the body as that of his youngest daughter.

Once the manhunt was underway, Alan Wills was on the run less than twenty-four hours. Late on Friday afternoon, as a result of very extensive inquiries, Wills was arrested in a house in Mawdesley village, near Croston, about 4.30 pm, by a PC Brown, of the Lancashire County Constabulary, and brought to Southport by Detective Inspector Geoff Wright, Detective Sergeant Maurice Mackenzie-Folan, and Detective Constable Peter Holmes. At the police station Wills made a statement (used in court) and was formally charged with the murder of Amanda Graham. Many more enquiries were made, and the Director of Public Prosecutions informed.

An inquest on Amanda was opened the same day (Friday afternoon) by the coroner for South West Lancashire, Mr Cornelius Bolton. He adjourned the inquest until 5 July, and expressed his sympathy to Amanda's parents for their 'tragic loss'.

In his statement following his arrest Wills said he remembered nothing after leaving the *Fisherman's Rest* pub (the only surviving part of the *Palace Hotel*), but added:

I am ashamed of everything I did.
I just woke up and seen her laid out on the bed.

The next morning (Saturday), seven minutes sufficed for the appearance of Wills, of no fixed address, to be remanded in custody, until Monday, 5 June, by Southport magistrates, accused of Amanda's murder between 24-25 May. The presiding magistrate was Mr W G Lithgow, who was sat with Dr W Limont, Miss I M Wood, and Miss Goodfellow.

There were not more than a dozen members of the public present when Wills, a small, thin, dark-skinned man with black hair and one eye partly closed, appeared in the dock, wearing a dark blue striped suit, no collar and his dark-coloured shirt was open at the neck. He was asked by the deputy magistrate, Mr E C Ball, if he had any objection to the remand, in a whisper that was just audible he said: 'No.'

The Chief Constable, Joseph Pessell, gave details of the deceased child.

Amanda's funeral took place early the following week and the service conducted by the Reverend W Cox, Vicar of Holy Trinity Church. Mr L Nutter, undertaker, had said the family wanted to keep the funeral as quiet as possible, without any sightseers.

The child murder case was heard at Liverpool Assizes, on Friday, 10 November 1961. The court heard that Mandy's body had been found in Wills' bedroom at the *Palace Hotel*, on the morning of 25 May, after she had been seen with Wills and had later been reported as missing the previous night.

Opening the case for the prosecution, on the Thursday, Mr Alexander Karmel, QC, leading the prosecution, outlined the facts of the case, which he described as 'shocking and horrific'.

It transpired that Mandy left Pleasureland about 7 pm and boarded a bus with her two friends. Wills was also a passenger on that bus, and when Amanda alighted in Leyland Road – one stop before her friends – Wills followed her. A witness saw them talking and another saw them walking down the road holding hands. The six year old seemed happy and carefree, smiling and engaged in conversation.

Just before 10 pm they were seen by a schoolgirl who knew them both, and asked Mandy why she wasn't at home at that time of night. Wills told the girl that he was taking Mandy home now, and they were watched walking in the right direction to Mandy's home, in Hartwood Road, just off the Manchester/Leyland Road junction.

'Unfortunately, members of the jury,' said Mr Karmel, 'Amanda was not taken home.'

Defending the prisoner, Mr Leslie Rigg, QC, said he was not in a position to contest the Crown's version of events as Wills had no recollection of carrying out the 'brutal act'. He therefore asked the jury to consider the state of Wills' mind at the time of the assault.

Medical evidence was called to support his suggestion that Wills – a grim loner who, it was led to be believed, had a child-like mind and attitude – was suffering from some mental illness. A hospital doctor, Dr Sharpe, said he had examined Alan Wills and found that in normal conversation he was cheerful, co-operative and apparently normal. However, he did possess a mental age of around eleven and was, in his opinion, borderline between 'definite sub normality' and 'the low average'.

Further medical evidence, from the senior medical officer at Liverpool's Walton prison, Dr Gray, told the court he felt that Wills was feigning illness, adding:

I formed the opinion that he knew more than he cared to admit or was willing to discuss about the events of 24 May.

As medical evidence took up the majority of the case, it was left to the judge, Mr Justice Atkinson, to summarise all the facts and explain the legal ramifications in regard to the medical conditions mentioned in court.

The judge, Mr Justice Fenton Atkinson, remarked that there was little doubt as to Wills' guilt, considering early statements he had made. He told the jury there were two separate issues, they had to decide if he was guilty as charged, or was suffering from diminished responsibility. They must consider whether he was fully responsible mentally for his actions; that he did in fact kill the child in such conditions that the crime was murder; or whether, by reason of his mental state, he was not, and therefore should not be held responsible for his actions. If it was the latter it would be a case of manslaughter.

Then, in one of the most dramatic summing ups ever heard in a court of law, Mr Justice Atkinson, referring to the medical evidence, asked the jury to consider if while carrying out the brutal sexual assault on his young victim Wills had intentionally strangled her. He said it had taken between fifteen and thirty seconds for the child to become asphyxiated through hard pressure on her throat, and said: 'Just let us see how long it is.' Holding his wristwatch in his hand he timed fifteen seconds. Complete silence hung heavy around the courtroom, until his lordship finally uttered to the jury:

> It is quite a long time. It is for you to decide if a man has forced intercourse with a child of six years of age, and then chokes her for fifteen seconds, would he have the understanding of what he was doing?

It took the jury of ten men and two women less than forty minutes to reach their decision at the end of the two-day trial, returning a verdict of guilty of murder. Announcing the sentence, Mr Justice Atkinson added:

> I pass the only sentence allowed by law – you will be imprisoned for life.

The strange-looking little man, who had pleaded not guilty, remained silent as he left the dock. With the words: 'You have been found guilty of a very terrible crime' ringing in his ears, the thirty-three-year-old hotel worker, Alan Victor Wills, was escorted from the dock to start a term of life imprisonment for the murder and molesting of Holy Trinity schoolgirl Amanda Graham.

Life for a life – but such a precious young life. It was a murder of innocence, and there hangs the debate; should the death penalty be brought back for child-killers? Despite heated campaigns practically every time a child is brutally murdered, monsters like Wills rot away in places like Walton gaol – becoming the second-longest detainee in the country serving life imprisonment.

In November 2007, Amanda's sister, Pauline Hadfield, of Manchester Road, told the *Champion* newspaper that she believed her young sister's spirit may have haunted the *Palace Hotel*. In 1963 a chambermaid said she repeatedly 'saw' Amanda.

Pauline said she had been working in Whitby at the time of the murder, and had to come back by train, adding, 'There were people reading the papers and it was all over the front pages'. Pauline was seventeen when Mandy died. She said, 'I can talk about it nowm, but I couldn't for a long time after. I still think about her everyday. She was a very cheerful girl, always laughing and talking to people'.

Murderer Alan Wills, knew Amanda through her older brother who worked as a chef at the *Palace Hotel*. Amanda may have been taken to Wills' room after being murdered in the lift, and some paranormal investigators believe it was then haunted by the little girl, a victim of a very real tragedy. Another incident was when the room where the six-year-old was molested and killed, inexplicably caught fire one night.

Pauline concluded, 'Such a lot of things happened at the hotel that makes you wonder whether there is something – but I would now like to think Amanda is at rest'.

Chapter 5

Murder of the Religious 'Pink Lady'
Derby Road
1971

*When a little grey-haired old lady was found strangled to death
in her Derby Road bed-sit one autumn afternoon, early
in October 1971, the police had to scratch around to
establish something about her. All they knew was
that she was known as the 'pink lady'.*

While detectives – led by Detective Superintendent Wilfred Brooks – admitted they lacked much background knowledge, the police investigation only discovered that the dead woman was someone the whole street did not know; neighbours in the normally quiet roadway only referred to her as '*The Pink Lady*,' due to her preference for that colour clothing and co-ordination.

Sixty-nine-year-old Maura McAndrew, a 5ft 4in tall woman, described as 'of good build,' had been found at 12.10 pm lying face-down on the floor (one report said on her bed), in her bedsitting room at the top of the house, 34 Derby Road, on Monday, 4 October; she had been strangled by the flex of her own electric kettle.

The alarm was raised by Mr and Mrs A E Hinton-Calcutt, of 32 Derby Road. The retired gent, who said 'the dead woman was a stranger to him' added:

An elderly woman called after 12 noon and reported her death. My wife called the police on our telephone. I never spoke to her, she kept herself to herself, although she was quite an active person and used to go out and about a lot. I last saw her on Saturday passing our gate.

The abode of the 'Pink Lady', 34 Derby Road. Sam Cookson

As usual, Maura was wearing a predominantly pink outfit – a pink and white coat and a pink hat – when she was last seen alive, leaving the Derby Road semi at about 3 pm on the Saturday afternoon.

Despite little being known of the mystery murder victim in the first few days, squads of detectives began hunting her killer, and officers from several of the North West Regional Task Forces were called in to help the Southport Division of the Lancashire Constabulary, and some sixty detectives were engaged on inquiries during the day, including investigations at the house, owned by Alfred Emett and his wife Jenny, who both lived there.

Derby Road was not exactly the Coronation Street of Southport. It was (then) a quiet roadway where no-one seemed to know other neighbours very well – and where nothing out of the ordinary ever happened.

Close to the town centre, the only activity and noise on a weekday was the coming and going of vehicles from the Corporation car park, the Children's Department, and the National Coal Board offices on the opposite side of the road from the murder scene – where Derby Road railway depot used to be, with Steamport Museum a little further up.

Since those days the hustle and bustle of Asda superstore keeps the roadway busy with traffic and there was a double murder in Derby Road in June 2002.

Back in the early 1970s, many of the houses in Derby Road had been divided into flats, but were mainly neat and tidy, the murder house itself particularly so. Painted blue and cream with a paved forecourt, the windows were draped with heavy net curtains. A resident living next door at No 36, said:

It is quiet down here during the week but we often hear a lot of drunkards on a Saturday night. We heard nothing suspicious at all, and our dog would have barked if there had been any noise.

It was a black day for two florist sisters who owned the flower shop directly across the road, only a few yards from the murder scene. Mrs Margaret Massam and Mrs Jean Sefton, of 1 Kensington Road, had just got back from a friend's funeral when they heard talk of the murder at No 34. Mrs Massam, who had never seen Maura McAndrew, said:

We wondered what was happening when there were police swarming all over the place. I knew Mr & Mrs Emett from when they used to live in the Marshside area. Mr Emett used to run a plumbing business. He's an invalid now. It always seems quiet here. It's a place where you don't know many people.

Two other neighbours said they didn't know the woman, although they were 'shocked' to hear of the news. One commented: 'I knew Mr & Mrs Emett, Mrs Emett's sister, the daughter, son-in-law and their baby, but I didn't know of anyone else living there.'

A post-mortem examination was carried out at Duke Street mortuary on the Tuesday by Dr John Gorden Benstead, the Home Office pathologist, in order to establish the time and cause of death. At 5 pm the previous

The Derby Road house at the time of the murder. Southport Visiter

day, Maura's brother was informed of his sister's death, and at 4.15 pm identified her body, at the mortuary, to PC Armfield.

Maura Mary McAndrew was born at the turn of the century, on 29 June 1902, at Largen, County Mayo. A single woman (spinster), she was a devout Roman Catholic, who attended St Marie's church, in Seabank Road. She had been there during the weekend before her death, although the senior priest, Father John Twomey, did not know her.

Maura, who is thought to have worked in the catering trade at some point, lived in Bournmouth for some years, and was a retired governess. She had recently returned from abroad, and had only been living in her Derby Road bed-sitting room for three months.

Later, in court, the judge said she was 'an eccentric old lady who said silly things'.

It didn't take the police very long to find the culprit, and they

St Marie's Church. Author's collection

didn't have to look very far. At 6.40 pm the same day of the murder, detectives making inquiries saw Brendan Leech in his apartment at the same address. At Southport police station he was interviewed by Detective Chief Inspector Ronnie Holt, second in command of Lancashire No 3 District Task Force, and Leech made a statement denying any knowledge of the deceased.

But at 6.35 am (one report says 6.15 am) on Wednesday, 6 October, Detective Chief Inspector Tom Davies and Inspector Holt, stopped Leech, a twenty-five-year-old labourer, in Old Park Lane, and cautioned him. Leech replied:

Jesus Christ, I didn't think you would come again so soon.

The two detectives took Leech to Southport police station, where Inspector Holt and Detective Superintendent Raymond Jackson questioned him about discrepancies in his original statement. He broke down in tears at one point, put his head in his hands and cried. Asked why he was crying, he said it was because they suspected him of the murder.

The detectives then left him for half-an-hour to collect himself. When they returned they told Leech forensic evidence showed that he was connected with the death. After sobbing again for a long time he relented and told them what really happened. At 10.45am Leech was formerly charged with the murder of Miss McAndrew. He replied: 'I am sorry; I didn't know what I was doing, I just saw red.'

The accused, a blond-haired man with a soft Irish brogue, appeared in court shortly before lunch that day, and remanded in custody for eight days, until Friday, 15 October. During the five minute hearing, before Mr J G Johnson, he said he was born in Dublin and met his wife there in 1968 when she was on holiday from Southport. Early in 1970 she became pregnant and left her Southport home to live with him in Dublin until the baby was born. They were married in 1971.

The couple came back to England and his wife's grandmother, Mrs J Emett, provided them with a home in her house at 34 Derby Road. A few months later, Miss McAndrew went to live at the house, in the top bed-sitter.

Brendan Leech said Miss McAndrew once suggested that he was

not a true Roman Catholic and was greedy for working on a Sunday. His wife told him that the old lady had said their baby was too big for its age, and that its great grandmother (Mrs Emmett) took it out more often than its own mother. Miss McAndrew also told Leech that the RC Church did not recognise mixed marriages and he would be excommunicated. He replied he was saving up to buy a house.

Wearing an open-necked plaid shirt, leather jacket and jeans, Leech listened calmly as the Southport magistrates' clerk, Mr Benjamin Hartwell, OBE, read the charge that:

On or about October 3, at Southport, he murdered Maura Mary McAndrew, against the Peace of our Sovereign Lady the Queen, her Crown, and Dignity.

Inspector Joe Sewell, prosecuting, applied for the remand, and DCI Holt gave evidence of Leech's arrest at 6.20 am; Leech did not apply for bail and was advised of his rights regarding legal aid.

Meanwhile, relatives of Miss McAndrew travelled to Southport from Birmingham and the South of England where they had been traced by the police, including Maura's brother, James McAndrew, a sixty-year-old master carpenter, of Yardley Wood, Birmingham.

The inquest was opened at Southport on Friday morning, 8 October, by Coroner G H Glasgow (brother of local historian Dr Eric Glasgow) for identification only, and adjourned until the next day.

At Liverpool Crown Court, on 24 January 1972, before Mr Justice Griffiths, the prosecuting counsel, Mr Michael Maguire, stated that a 'religious war of words' led to the death of Miss McAndrew.

During the opening of the murder trial, Brendan Leech pleaded not guilty to murder, but guilty to manslaughter. He contended that Maria provoked him by criticising him, his wife, their marriage and, finally, their thirteen-month old daughter, Sharon.

Leech had told the police that on the previous day, a Sunday, he went out about 11.55 am and had six or seven pints of ale at three public houses. He returned home about 2 pm, but did not go into the house, instead he threw stones up at his flat window to see if his wife was in. There was no response so he assumed she had already gone to her mother's at High Park, where they went every Sunday, so he followed by bus.

However, his wife had told police that when Leech arrived at her mother's High Park home, he said he had walked all the way.

Another tenant at 34 Derby Road, had also said that she saw Leech in the house about 2 pm that day.

Leech's original statement was that he did not enter the house when he returned to his flat at 2 pm on 3 October, when he found that his teenage wife, Pauline, had gone out.

Instead, he said, the lady from upstairs (Miss McAndrew) opened her door and told him that his wife had gone out, and then asked him if he fancied a cup of coffee, so he went up to her room. He sat on the bed and she started to make the coffee, and said:

Do you know you are not properly married, you being a Catholic and your wife being Church of England, a Protestant?

She then asked which faith his baby was being brought up, and he replied they had sorted that out, it was to be in his wife's faith. Miss McAndrew objected to that, saying it was not the right religion, and said that if anything happened to his daughter she would not go to heaven. Leech added:

She kept on about this and about my working on a Sunday. She said she had told the wife's grandmother downstairs, the priest and other people she knew about the three of us living in sin. I think she had made the coffee by this time. She went on about my wife and I arguing and she was inquiring about our relationship. I don't know whether she was standing up or not but she turned away from me, and said, 'anyway, the baby's a bastard; she was born before you were married.'

When she said that I saw red, and I lost my head. I picked up an electric flex from the floor and put it around her neck from behind. I pulled it tight and she fell to the floor and she was kicking and struggling. I pulled the flex tighter and knotted it around her neck. I moved away from her and then realised what I had done. I did not know whether she was dead or not so I poured water from the kettle on to her legs, to try and revive her with the shock, but she did not move, so I knew she was dead.

He then ran out of the door, leaving it open, and went for the High Park bus.

In court Leech said he did not actually recollect choking her with the flex; it was only when she sank to the floor that he realised what he had done. Cross-examined by Mr Maguire, he said he did not think drink was at all responsible for his actions.

Defence counsel, Mr David McNeil, called four witnesses to give character sketches of the old lady.

Mr Roy Marsden, an executive officer of the Department of Health and Social Security in Southport, said she came over from Ireland and was 'disgruntled' with her accommodation, and that she was 'highly strung, unsettled and at odds with the world'.

Mrs Elizabeth Lowry, of 42 Pilkington Road, Southport, a daughter of Mrs Emett, said Miss McAndrew often said the baby was far too fat and criticised young Mrs Leech for not bringing the baby up properly, and said Miss McAndrew talked a lot of nonsense.

Mrs Jennie Finlayson, another daughter of Mrs Emett said of the old lady:

She was malicious, and out to cause trouble. She was frequently pulling baby Sharon to pieces, saying she was not brought up properly or fed properly. She said everywhere was filthy dirty and she could not walk out in the streets without getting contaminated.

Mrs Pauline Leech told the court:

Miss McAndrew said Sharon was not a Christian and that I was not married in the eyes of the Church. She also criticised the way I brought her up. She got me down.

Summing up for the defence, Mr Maguire said that Miss McAndrew's behaviour in the few weeks before her death was consistent with her behaviour as described by the defendant in the last few minutes of her life. He submitted that it was not a planned or motivated murder, but that the accused was provoked and attacked her spontaneously.

When the case opened on the Monday afternoon, two witnesses were called for the prosecution, and both gave similar accounts of Miss McAndrew.

Mrs Jenny Emett, of the same address, who found the body and gave evidence of identification, said Miss McAndrew annoyed her with her talk about Protestants not being Christian. Miss Howard, also of that address, said Miss McAndrew kept coming into her flat and annoying her, adding:

She called people wicked if they were Protestants. She said Southport was a dirty place and people were nasty to talk to her. She was always criticising the baby's mother and the baby because they were not Roman Catholics. I think she hated the baby.

The judge ruled that the jury had to consider whether a rational man would have done this in these circumstances.

After a trial which had lasted just five hours, the jury of eleven men and one woman took half-an-hour to reach its unanimous verdict. Found 'guilty' of murdering the sixty-nine-year-old spinster, Brendan Joseph Christopher Leech was jailed for life.

As soon as it was announced, Mrs Pauline Leech, the accused's nineteen-year-old wife, screamed 'No, no' and was led out of the court room at St George's Hall, Liverpool.

'Pink Lady' murder trial:

Wife screams as husband is found guilty of murder

Pink Lady murder trial:

'Saw red' when his baby was called a bastard

Two newspaper cuttings showing the headlines this murder case made
Southport Visiter

Chapter 6

Death of a Lonely Moneylender
Alexandra Road
1975

*When loner Stanley Prescott was discovered in his pyjamas,
laying in a pool of blood, slumped behind a door, more
than eighty detectives were quickly drafted into the massive
murder hunt for his killer. Being a money man, the elderly
gent was the prime target for a callous thug, who
fractured his skull and ransacked his home.*

Lonely widower Stanley Prescott had continued his trade as a credit draper on a part-time basis after retiring to Southport in 1966. Working mainly in the Manchester area, the sixty-seven-year-old was a moneylender, which often required him to have cash available – which made him a tempting target for any thug who knew this.

*Murder victim
Stanley Prescott.*
Southport Visiter

Mr Prescott lived alone, he liked it that way. He was a quiet man with very few friends. He lived in an apartment on the third floor, a top flat, within a large Victorian house at 51 Alexandra Road – believed to have been the *Alexandra Hotel* at one time. Stanley Prescott retired to this 'peaceful resort' nine years previously, and had been in his flat for eight years.

On Wednesday, 19 December 1975, at about 10.30 pm the house caretaker for the block of flats, Frederick Usher, became worried when he found a small black cash box lying smashed open on the stairs, and realized it was Mr Prescott's. The box contained about £5 worth of old coinage. He ventured up to the top landing and heard groaning noises coming from the inside hallway of Mr Prescott's apartment.

Mr Usher immediately went to call the police. When they arrived they forced open Mr Prescott's locked door, and found him unconscious, dying on the floor behind his door. He had fractures of the skull, jaw, facial bones and two ribs. The seventy-six-year-old caretaker said 'he looked as if he had been washing himself in blood'.

Mr Prescott was rushed to Southport Infirmary with severe head injuries. Detectives kept a constant vigil by his hospital bedside hoping he would recover to tell them about the brutal attack – but he finally lost his battle for life at 6 am on the Friday morning. The injuries to his head were so severe he died from cerebral haemorrhage. The police would not say whether he regained consciousness before he died.

During the week before Christmas 1975 Merseyside Police launched a massive hunt for his killer. Detective Superintendent Walter Givan, who led the initial inquiries, said extra police officers were called in because of the serious nature of the crime. More than eighty detectives were drafted in from all over the region to help, and the head of Merseyside CID, Tommy Whittlestone, then took over the investigation.

Det Con Walter Givan. Southport Visiter

A special incident room was set up at Southport Police Station on the Thursday morning and detectives immediately began the task of trying to trace relatives and friends of Mr Prescott, while forensic experts combed his two-bedroom flat for any possible clues. The flat, No 8, which had been ransacked, was then padlocked by the police.

The dead man's closest relatives lived in Spain, but a son-in-law, Karl Rowcroft, happened to be in Britain on business and he was brought to Southport on the Friday (19 December) to formally identify Mr Prescott; the post-mortem was carried out by the Home Office pathologist Dr John Gordon Benstead.

Superintendent Gordon Mackenzie, deputy head of Merseyside CID, said it seemed likely Mr Prescott had lain dying in his flat for several hours before he was discovered. He appealed to anyone who may have seen anything suspicious between 1 pm and 3 pm on the

Victorian villa, 51 Alexandra Road, home of murdered Stanley Prescott. Southport
Visiter

previous Wednesday to come forward, adding: 'From the inquiries
we have made it seems clear this is the critical time.'

Detectives spent two days interviewing all residents in the
immediate area of Alexandra Road, and also contacted customers
of Mr Prescott's credit drapery business both in Southport and
Manchester. One resident in the house had noticed something
suspicious – the abandoned cash box on the stairs when he returned
from work just after 4.30 pm – six hours before Mr Prescott was
found – but he didn't do anything about it. If he had then perhaps
Mr Prescott would have survived the vicious attack.

This was, in fact, the second robbery in a year at Mr Prescott's flat – but unfortunately on this occasion he was still at home.

The police traced two male GPO television licence department officials who were in the area at the time of death; they were interviewed but later ruled out of the inquiries.

Neighbours within the Alexandra Road house described Stanley as a quiet man with few friends. Neither the caretaker nor his wife, Lillian, had been inside the top-floor flat during the eight years he had lived there. Mr Usher said:

He was a loner and kept himself to himself. He never had any visitors. Nobody ever really saw him, and he even left notes outside his door if he wanted extra deliveries of coal – so we never had to disturb him.

Mr Prescott's work often took him to Manchester for the whole day twice a week and he would usually spend the following day in bed. He had only just recovered from a heart attack which put him in the nearby Promenade Hospital for four weeks during the summer.

So, what happened that day?

Being hard up (as usual) and finding life was hard with no work, part-time petty thief and house burglar, Keith Weatherall, of Alexandra Road, spent some time being driven around Southport by his girlfriend, Miss Alma McCoy, secretly looking at ideal homes – to rob.

At about 2.30 pm Weatherall's girlfriend dropped him off in a taxi in the vicinity of his Alexandra Road flat. Back at his flat he paced the floor wondering where he could get some money from. It then 'came back to him about the old man down the road who had a few bob', and decided to go and have a look.

The unemployed twenty-eight-year-old walked up the stairs to the top of the building, and knocked on the door of Mr Prescott's flat. There was no answer and so he got his screwdriver out, but then noticed the door was ajar. He walked in, thinking the old man had forgotten to lock the door, and went straight to the cupboard where the money was last time. He then heard a little noise in the kitchenette, like the plug coming out of a kettle. As he walked in he came face-to-face with Mr Prescott. Weatherall, who was far more startled than Mr Prescott, panicked and attacked the old man. In his words he said:

I was holding my screwdriver in my hand at this time and the handle was sticking up out of my hand. I swiped at him and hit him on the head, the side of the head and the top of the head. He fell straight down and there was a bang as he hit the floor. I stood there staring at him for a couple of minutes. I think he was knocked out, because his head hit the floor as well, but he was breathing all right and moaning. There was no sign of blood or anything. I thought he'd be all right but I'd have time to get the money before he came round. I went into the living room and got the money out of the cupboard. I went out of the house and down the road towards my flat. I didn't realize the extent of what I had done and I didn't think that it would turn out like it did because I am not a violent person. I'm sorry that I ever went in the place and I'll always regret what I've done.

When the poor man's death was reported in the press and on television, Weatherall told Miss McCoy not to say he had been in Southport with her at that time. Not surprisingly, Weatherall lied to the police when questioned a few days after Mr Prescott's death, saying he had nothing to do with the murder, but then admitted he was there, but this became 'he was already injured and lying on the floor when I got there'.

Later, Weatherall said that the main room was in a tip, and as he went to a cupboard he heard a click like a plug coming out of a socket. He went and looked and found Mr Prescott lying face down on the floor. (So who made the click?) He then said he went into the living room to have a look around, then the bedroom, where nothing seemed to be untidy or missing. He left, using the stairs and came out running part of the way down the road, until he saw his girlfriend, Alma. Not the tightest of defences.

The police had been unable to establish a link between this incident and the previous one – until Weatherall confessed. Questioned by the police, he admitted he had previously burgled Mr Prescott's flat and stolen more than £200 in February the previous year.

Keith Weatherall made a three minute court appearance during the Christmas week, when Chief Superintendent Frank Jones, Head of Merseyside Police 'H' Division, asked the chairman of North Sefton magistrates, Lieutenant Colonel George Appleton for Weatherall to be remanded, which he duly was; he was not legally represented but applied for legal aid. Reporting restrictions were not lifted during the hearing.

Weatherall was also charged with stealing £245 from Mr Prescott between 3 and 4 February 1974. Put on remand, the nasty piece of work spent the first of many Christmas's behind the bars of Risley Prison, and without his girlfriend. He then appeared before North Sefton magistrates on Tuesday, 30 December 1975, charged with the murder of Stanley Prescott. He pleaded not guilty to murder, and so was committed for trial at Liverpool Crown Court, on Friday, 12 April 1976. The trial, before Judge Sir Rudolph Lyons, QC, Recorder of Liverpool, was expected to last three days. Mr Norman Miscampbell was prosecuting along with Mr Herbert Andrew.

On the third day of the trial, Weatherall went into the witness box and stubbornly denied the allegation that he murdered Mr Prescott, despite having given a full admission statement to Detective Sergeant John Fletcher who read it out to the jury. Detective Constable Daniel Gidman also told the court that under interview Weatherall admitting hitting Mr Prescott.

Weatherall was sentenced on 13 April 1976, for what the judge described as: 'the callous and brutal murder of an elderly man occupying a flat he was burgling at the time'. The Recorder (judge) said the law provided only one sentence for murder – imprisonment for life.

Chapter 7

Bathtub Murder of Gay Shopkeeper
Abram's Fold, Banks
1986

The brutal murder of an inoffensive shoe shop owner,
Nigel Bostock, who was strangled and stabbed six times
and found slumped over the side of a bath, after a Christmas
party at home, has never been solved. The thirty-something
gay man was also robbed of £700, gold rings and an expensive
and distinctive wristwatch – but was he the victim of a
'snuff' video? This puzzling case featured on Crimewatch UK.

T he sadistic slaying of Nigel Bostock in his own home, is probably the most baffling murder mysteries in Southport's history. It has now chalked up a macabre twenty years with detectives still no nearer to solving the horrible crime. His semi-naked, bloodstained body was found slumped over the side of his bathtub, but police operations to find the culprits have only been met by a veil of silence from the 'gay underworld'.

Nigel Samuel Bostock was pretty well known in the gay fraternity; being a practicing homosexual he frequented North West gay clubs. With regular excursions between Liverpool and Blackpool, he was described as 'a homosexual with a wide circle of friends'.

He had lived alone in his tidy semi-detached dormer bungalow, 10 Abram's Fold, a secluded cul-de-sac in the small

Nigel Bostock. Southport Champion

Mr Bostock's Wesley Street shoe shop. Southport Champion

village community of Banks just outside Southport, for two years, and owned a specialist shoe shop in Southport's town centre.

The thirty-one-year-old was described by family and friends as being a very nice, sensitive person, friendly and well liked, with a kind and gentle nature. He socialised, but was a shy person. His death was catastrophic for his family, some of whom were away on holiday in the Lake District when this terrible murder was committed.

On the day he was killed – just five days before Christmas – Nigel had been out for lunch with his parents. He was last seen leaving his shop, no 6 Wesley Street, at 2 pm (some reports say 4 pm) on Friday, 19 December 1986; he drove his red Ford Fiesta car (reg no CEC 325) to his bungalow for a pre-arranged meeting with a central heating engineer, who was the last known person to see him alive. The repair man called at 5.20 pm, but what exactly occurred over the next eighteen hours, including the evening and night he was murdered, remains a mystery.

What is known is that when he failed to arrive at his footwear shop, just off Eastbank Street, by lunchtime the next day (Saturday, 20 December), his female assistant telephoned a friend, but couldn't get through, so 'phoned a neighbour friend of his about 12.30 pm'; concerned, the man forced entry into Nigel's bungalow, climbed through a kitchen window and found his bludgeoned body at 12.50 pm.

Colleagues at Wesley Footwear – the Wider Fitting Shoe Specialists – were too upset to talk. Freda, the manageress who lived over the shop, was especially close to Nigel; she washed, ironed and mothered him, and they regularly went out for meals together.

Nigel was discovered slumped 'half-in and half-out of his bathtub'. An electric blanket cord used to strangle him was still wrapped around his neck – but these details weren't released to reporters at the time. Neither was the fact that cannabis was found in the lounge.

After the thirty-something-year-old had been brutally strangled, he was then stabbed six times in the chest and stomach with a kitchen knife – three of the wounds were considerably deep. Evidence suggested Nigel was strangled in his bedroom and then taken into the bathroom. Once there, the killer tried to electrocute him – hence the shallow bath of water?

Lancashire Police worked on the theory that Mr Bostock was visited by up to four people, probably from the Lancashire gay clubs he frequented, for a small, cosy, Christmas party. Exactly who these people were is still a mystery and the police, to this day, would like to speak to a man called Carl (or Karl) believed to have been Nigel's boyfriend. It appeared that the murdered man knew his assailants, as there was no sign of a break-in or of a struggle. Detectives believe there could have been more than one murderer.

It was discovered that Nigel Bostock spread his wings wide in the homosexual world, and regularly took people with homosexual tendencies back to his house. The gay scene was apparently too quiet in Southport, with nowhere to go at that time, so he usually ventured further afield. However, his favourite pub was the *Fox & Goose*, in Cable Street, where bikers and gays mixed happily together, neither threatening to the other.

However, it came as a surprise to many that Nigel was gay,

Nigel's bungalow in Abram's Fold where he was murdered following a sex act that went horribly wrong. Southport Visiter

despite him subtly 'cruising' the area for a couple of years. He was a quiet, friendly, inoffensive person – and a private one. He hadn't told anyone in his family about his sexuality; his closet was tightly closed.

Police officers and detectives made a fingertip search of the murder scene, and then some 750 people were seen during door-to-door inquiries in the Banks area. A mobile police station was set up in Abram's Fold, with an incident room at Hutton Hall, Preston, and then members of Southport's gay community were questioned.

Detectives may have been baffled by this hideous crime, but they didn't need to be brain surgeons to realise there had been a small gathering of people round for drinks, as there were several empty beer cans and lots of cigarettes in an ashtray. Some beer can ring-pulls were also found in Nigel's car – which had remained untouched in the driveway throughout.

During the house-to-house calls a few people reported noises and raised voices just hours before the murder, but immediate neighbours neither saw nor heard anyone arrive or leave Nigel's usually quiet bungalow; so how did the visiting killer/s leave the scene without being spotted? A police spokesperson said:

> *The public, press and especially the homosexual community, have been very co-operative during our investigations, but there are many puzzles still to be solved. The people living in the adjoining semi to Mr Bostock's house gave a totally conflicting statement to the people living opposite the house.*

The people living next door to Mr Bostock said they heard the sound of a scuffle at 11.30 pm, which they described as someone being dragged across the floor, while the people living opposite said Nigel went out in his little red car at 9.45 pm. There was no reason to disbelieve either of the neighbours as Mr Bostock could easily have gone out, picked someone up and brought them back home.

At a press conference at Hutton, Detective Superintendent John Boyd, second in command at Lancashire CID, leading the murder hunt, said:

Det Supt John Boyd. Southport Visiter

> *There may be more than one killer and I am quite certain that when Mr Bostock opened the door on Friday evening he knew his visitors. We have conflicting reports about him being at home and being out, but the estimated time of death was late Friday night or early Saturday morning. We found address books, diaries and pieces of paper with names and addresses. Our enquiries are at an advanced stage, after interviewing what I consider to be his inner circle of friends, but we believe there is a wider circle. Nigel had picked up quite a few people and taken them home, and there have been steady relationships with a number of people. We have interviewed one of his friends with AIDS but we know that Mr Bostock did not have the AIDS virus.*

We should like people who knew Mr Bostock to contact us – in confidence if they like. We desperately need to know his movements on Friday evening and we certainly need to know the movements of other people who have visited him. There are indications that people had been having a social drink at the bungalow. We are trying to trace motor vehicles or people who have been there.

With the lead up to Christmas, Lancashire detectives deployed fifty detectives to comb and scour the gay underworld from Liverpool to Blackpool hunting for those involved in the vile killing. Nightclubs and pubs used by homosexuals and those Mr Bostock were known to have frequented, at Southport, Preston, Liverpool, Bolton and Blackpool, were all infiltrated.

The police quickly established that the knifed businessman had also been robbed of cash and jewellery items; between £600-£700 was taken from a briefcase that had been forced open - probably the proceeds from the shoe shop, which he hadn't banked. However, it was learnt that Nigel never used a safe for his shop takings, in fact, he took them home every night - and put them in his fridge. Freezing his assets? The killer may have known that.

Also stolen was a very unusual and distinctively styled Bulova Accutron 'Spaceview' wristwatch, with a transparent face displaying the electronic mechanism behind the hands; the stainless steel back casing was on a gold-plated heavy-link bracelet strap. It was a rare watch, with only about 150 having been sold in the UK.

Nigel Bostock's distinctive watch and bracelet that were stolen after he was murdered. Champion newspaper

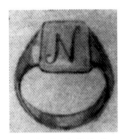

Nigel's initialled ring which also went missing. Southport Champion

Two nine-carat gold rings were also part of the expensive haul; one was described as a well-worn gent's signet ring with the initial 'N' inscribed on the front; the other being a dress ring with twenty-eight small diamonds in two rows across the front. These items became vital clues in this murder hunt, but police knew they may have been taken to make it look like a robbery.

On Christmas Day, in an effort to track down the killer or killers, Nigel's parents issued a 'substantial reward' for information leading to the arrest and conviction of whoever was responsible for their son's death.

A week on, the police had failed to uncover the stolen items; and a brown Mk III Ford Cortina, with a noisy exhaust blowing badly - reported to have been heard and seen being driven down Lancaster Drive, turning into Station Road towards Preston, at about 2.15 am on Saturday - was eventually eliminated from the inquiry. This crime proved to be a difficult nut to crack.

In January 1987, police had still not discounted the possibility that the murderer may be a local man. More than fifty officers were still engaged in inquiries. Pictures and descriptions of the stolen property had been distributed, and Detective Superintendent Boyd said they had been interviewing known Southport homosexuals. He added:

We are also interviewing people called Carl, who match the description of a hitch-hiker people believe Mr Bostock took back to his home. We still want to trace this man who is thought to be in his early 20s with reddish or sandy coloured hair.

This was to be the most mysterious part of all; as the victim's close friend, Carl or Karl, was known to have associated with Mr Bostock - thought to be a relationship - for at least two years; he had certainly visited the Abram's Fold home on several occasions, including in the months prior to the murder. He was one of several men who had still not been traced, in spite of all the publicity.

January also saw police stage a reconstruction of the 8.20 pm Southport to Liverpool train journey Nigel made two days before (Thursday, 18 December) his death, in the hope of identifying a party of three young men a witness saw him sharing a carriage with; they were roughly the same age as the murdered businessman, all dressed smartly, but casual. They all got off at Sandhills station. Unfortunately, this reconstruction revealed nothing.

Despite a swift public response in the early stages of the murder hunt, at the beginning of the New Year detectives appeared to have hit a wall of silence. Calls and information tailed off and no new leads were unearthed; they feared the trail may have gone cold. A Lancashire Police spokesperson said:

We have been disappointed in the lack of feed-back we have been getting. Initially, we had more than twenty calls from people who were very helpful, but as time goes on we are receiving less and less.

So, DS Boyd pinned his hopes on a new line of enquiry - officers interviewed people with convictions of blackmail and offences using violence, saying:

If any members of the gay community have been threatened with violence, either at home or in the streets, and money has been demanded from them, I would like to hear from them, in confidence. I would also like to remind the public that Mr Bostock's family are still prepared to offer a substantial reward for information that leads to the arrest, or conviction, of the person or persons involved.

Millions of television viewers heard an appeal for help when the 'Bostock case' was featured on the BBC's *Crimewatch UK* programme (Tuesday, 29 January). The show included a plea by detectives for people to be on the lookout for the items stolen from the house the night Mr Bostock was murdered. Specific details of electric flex tied by the killer were also revealed during a reconstruction of the murder.

The useful slot on the popular programme was successful in that it revealed new leads. Police telephone lines at the London studios and Lancashire Constabulary headquarters were jammed with more than sixty calls (thirty-two of them by the Crimewatch Incident Desk).

A Torquay man, called Philip, had his call cut off or hung up after

Lancashire Police Reinvestigate Murder of Gay Man from 1986

£5,000 Reward

from CRIMESTOPPERS for information leading to a conviction

Nigel Bostock (31), a gay man, was found dead at his home address on Abrams Fold in Banks on Saturday 20th December 1986, he had been strangled and stabbed.

Watch BBC's Crimewatch on Tuesday, 21 September

If you have any information please contact the incident room on 01695 566566

A reward poster – but nobody benefitted from it. Lancashire Police

saying he had information on the distinctive 'see-through' watch. Another caller said he had information on Nigel's friend Carl, claiming he was a relative. He also described Carl as being white, aged early twenties, of slim build with reddish or sandy coloured collar-length hair. Detective Superintendent John Boyd, the man in charge of the case, said afterwards:

> *I was very encouraged by the weight of calls from all over the country, and now have fifty-plus Lancashire detectives working on the case, many of them following up information received since the Crimewatch programme.*

Nearly thirty other police forces around the country were now involved, including Devon Constabulary who tried to trace the man called Philip. The police also brought in a sexual crime expert. The post-mortem indicates Nigel had had sex just before he was murdered.

On Friday, 27 February 1987, the *Liverpool Echo* reported that murder squad detectives had vetted more than 5,000 people over this unsolved, savage crime; DS Boyd said very intensive inquiries were still continuing, with 1,000 statements having been taken, as well as widespread publicity.

Home Office pathologist Dr John Burns said Nigel Bostock, a bachelor, died from ligature strangulation and a single stab wound in the chest. The body was identified by a nephew, Colin Bleasdale, of Tarn House, Parrs Lane, Aughton, who said his uncle had enjoyed reasonably good health. The inquest was adjourned but coroner Howard McCann issued an order allowing the funeral to take place. When the inquest was resumed in July 1987, at Preston, a verdict of 'unlawful killing' was recorded on Nigel Bostock.

By May 1987 nearly 1,400 statements had been taken, as the police sifted through the results of thorough investigations. Two 'Christmas card' friends called Reg and Doris (Hob?) were eliminated from the inquiry - although the mysterious third figure, Carl, Nigel's alleged boyfriend remained elusive.

Despite the new appeal on Crimewatch, another blank was drawn. But DS Boyd was still confident that the killers were still in the area and known within the gay underworld. He said the police had made extensive enquiries, contacted gay counselling lines and forty nightclubs, adding, at some length:

Despite the investigations slowing down to an extent during the last few months, we are still convinced that the offence was committed by one or more members of the local homosexual fraternity and that is where we will continue to focus our enquiries. We are certain that Mr Bostock's killer or killers were known to him on the night he was murdered and we have every reason to believe that they are still in the area. There is little cause to feel that they may have changed their haunts or way of life since the murder, yet if there is anyone who is known to have faded from the scene in the last few months, we would urge people to let us know. Mr Bostock had many business associates before his death due to his involvement in the shoe retail trade so it is likely that he knew many people in Southport, both gay and otherwise.

Despite a largely abortive six month search, which saw detectives taking 1,612 statements and interviewing 5,241 people - 924 of whom had been homosexual men, DS Boyd remained convinced that the killer would eventually be brought to justice. He confidently added:

I will always believe that we can catch the killer. We have covered a lot of ground, especially within the homosexual community, who are deeply alarmed at the murder, and I am convinced that one day one of them will tell us who is responsible. This is a murder which will not be forgotten, especially by the people of Banks.

December 1987 brought a fair bit of newspaper coverage, with the murder mystery and suspense case being a year old, and the dragnet for the killer clocking up its tragic first anniversary. At first senior detectives thought the case could be cleared up quickly, but it was not to be. Brain-scratching DS Boyd - who led twenty-six murder hunts in Lancashire during 1987, said:

The scene didn't appear baffling when we arrived, and we thought it would soon come to a satisfactory conclusion. But as the inquiry progressed, several puzzles emerged. I am sure it was a sexual act that went horribly wrong, but there was no need for Nigel to be stabbed and strangled, and we don't know why there was a small amount of water in the bath.

The police had been left puzzled in knowing how the killer (and accomplices?) left the isolated area. The shoe shop proprietor's car was in the driveway when the murder was discovered and no-one reported seeing any unusual cars in the area.

However, DS Boyd confirmed there would be no let up and pledged the killer would be caught - it was just a matter of time. He was certain that one of the people downstairs will not be able to continue carrying the burden of knowledge and will have to talk, adding:

Someone is going to tell us about it one day. You don't forget about something like this, or put it out of your mind. I frequently search my mind, but we are all equally certain there was nothing more we could have done. People coming into custody for homosexual-related offences are still being questioned about the murder. We have certainly made a tremendous depth of enquiry and over a very wide range in our hunt for the killers. I have always believed that there was more than one person involved. The scene indicated there were three or more people present. Usually when you find your motive for the crime you find your answer and there is no doubt that the motive for the visit of the offenders was sex.

And so the Nigel Bostock murder file remained open, bulging with information from interviews collected in the painstaking investigation. If the Abrams Fold resident knew his gruesome killers then there is a possibility that friends of his, who have not yet been identified, also knew his killers. But where and who is the elusive Carl?

Two unsuccessful years on, the police were still looking for Nigel's killer or killers, and mystery still shrouded what exactly happened at his home on the night of the murder.

It had clearly become a frustrating situation for the man heading the enquiry, DS Boyd, and yet he was still confident and adamant that the murder would not be forgotten, and was swift to refute press suggestions that they may have adopted a 'soft' attitude towards the case:

The evidence of the workload that has been involved and the number of officers connected would totally vindicate this. I have been involved in many murder cases and all are treated equally. I am not pessimistic. There seems to be more murders being solved now than in previous years; I'm sure this will be the case with Nigel's.

It wasn't until March 1989 that the police chief, desperate for clues to the grisly and mysterious Christmas-time death of the Banks man, made a fresh plea for information, after saying the murder squad would never give up. Two months later shocked murder squad detectives revealed that they had uncovered a seedy gay underworld in the North West, and the mystified crime bosses believed the public's attitude to 'gays' may have helped the sadistic killer evade justice, but hoped changing times would help them produce a vital breakthrough. They blamed a lack of public sympathy and the shadowy life of gays for blocking the final clues. Detective Sergeant Mike Pacey said:

Often homosexuals are married and bisexual so they are very reluctant to come forward. It's a shady, seedy world they live in and they are often subject to blackmail and violence. Homosexuals are often mugged and beaten up but they rarely complain to the police. Some of the people we come into contact with were highly respectable professionals - it really opened our eyes.

Several people were still being sought by the police, but still no-one had identified anyone. DCI Tony Gudgeon added:

If it was a child killer, we would have a lot of public interest and help. But this happened when the Aids scare broke and there was very little public sympathy for gays. In fact, Mr Bostock's post-mortem examination had to be delayed for twelve hours for an Aids check, but he didn't have it. Maybe now things have settled down, someone could come forward who wanted to keep a low profile at the peak of the operation. Obviously, the longer it goes on the less chance there is of finding a breakthrough.

In a blood-curdling twist to this murder mystery, the police strongly suggested that Nigel Bostock's death followed some kind of bizarre homosexual practice, which they've never specified; it appears that he was involved in a sex act that went horribly wrong. During the sexual play, which was apparently 'very evident and ferocious', the killer was sexually very violent, and Nigel was viciously and fatally bludgeoned, while practically nude - naked from the waist down, wearing just a short T-shirt. Some reports then referred to the culprit as 'the sex bath killer'.

On the three-year mark the man leading this murder inquiry was Detective Superintendent John Ashton, second-in-command at Lancashire CID. He said:

> *We will never give up until we have found the killer. It's only recently that we cleared up a twelve-year old murder case. We will continue to keep matters open.*

The next time this case was mentioned was five years later. With the killer still on the loose, and the mystery man Carl - who could have held the key to this gruesome murder - never traced, Detective Chief Inspector Graham White told the *Southport Visiter*:

> *The murder file remains open. Anything that does come in we will of course investigate, but in recent times information has been extremely sparse. A lot of work went into the Bostock investigation and the enquiry into his death is still on-going by police in the southern division.*

Nothing happened until June 1993, when Scotland Yard detectives, hunting a crazed serial killer preying on gay men in London, widened their net to probe possible links with Nigel's murder, nearly seven years earlier. Their visit here followed the death of Merseyside-born West End theatre director Peter Walker, the first victim of the serial killer. The naked body of the forty-five-year-old homosexual, who had been suffocated or strangled, was found at his flat in Battersea on 10 March, and the Metropolitan Police did not rule out a link, so travelled to Lancashire to liaise with officers. A spokesman said there was a big probability that Mr Walker and Mr Bostock had met, and that there were, without doubt, similarities between the two cases, after it emerged that Peter Walker originally came from Banks. Nigel's body had actually been discovered by Paul Walker, the brother of Peter Walker. However, both forces came to the conclusion that there was nothing solid to link the two cases. Detective Chief Inspector John Thornley said:

We compared notes in relation to the Bostock case and their investigations in London, particularly that of Peter Walker. Although he had a brother who was a friend of Nigel Bostock, this is just purely a coincidence. Enquiries are still on-going regarding our offence. Even after seven years there can be developments.

The next instalment was a disturbing one. In January 1995, the police believed the murdered shoe business man could have been a victim of a serial killer making so-called snuff videos - movies that involve real-life torture and murder of a person in front of a film crew.

The Metropolitan Police had launched a probe into allegations that a serial killer murdered several young homosexual men in the Merseyside area. The Obscene Publications Squad investigated the claims after being given details of murders and the name of an alleged serial killer, including details of burial sites in the area, but no link turned up here.

Then, five months later (June) trading standards officers seized 153 alleged snuff horror videos - the biggest ever in the borough - in a 'dawn raid' on a twenty-seven-year-old man's one-bedroom flat in central Southport, but no evidence of such revolting material was found from the haul, only simulated special effects of human deaths. Some of these 'video nasties' were banned from public viewing under the 1984 Video Recording Act, as they contained shocking scenes of violence, cannibalism, necrophilia, bestiality and torture. The police confiscated them all, saying they were 'horrific'.

Despite trading standards officers' attempts to curb the distribution of 'snuff' videos, the Britsh Board of Film Classification said, in 1993, that they have not reported a single case of such material anywhere in the British Isles.

But two years later, in early January 1995, the snuff video theory reared its ugly head again. Lancashire Police and Scotland Yard investigated new claims that Nigel Bostock was the victim of a gang making such videos. Several national newspapers carried details of snuff movie claims made by a Merseyside man. In the newspaper allegations the man said he was forced to trawl seafront arcades for lonely young males to lure back to a local house. There, he said, they were mutilated and murdered by a gang of perverts while video cameras recorded the gruesome events.

Nigel Bostock was said to be among the gang's victims, but no proof of this has surfaced.

In October 2001, Lancashire Police believed they were a step closer to finding the shopkeeper's murderer, and renewed their appeal for information about the now fifteen-year-old homicide. Police were still eager to trace the man in his twenties named Carl, believed to be from the Banks or Southport area. Inspector Martin Worden, of Lancashire Police, said:

We recovered a lot of forensic evidence at the scene and that was examined. However, technology has come on in leaps and bounds, we are constantly reviewing this evidence in the hope that it may lead to the identification of Nigel's killers, with evidence we can put before the court. There has been quite an encouraging response to our latest appeal, particularly in tracing Carl, who we believe was Nigel's boyfriend at the time of his death, and the weeks leading up to it. It shows there are people out there who are interested in Nigel's death but, more importantly, people who are interested in helping us find the person responsible for his death.

On 8 February 2002, a regional TV appeal was broadcast on ITV's *Case Unsolved* programme with a short reconstruction of the events leading up to Nigel's fatal stabbing and strangulation.

Two more years went by and then, in October 2003, detectives re-opened the investigation. With the development of modern DNA testing, items that had been gathered at the scene and stored, awaiting advances in technology, could now be prepared and sent for a fresh forensic review. Items examined included clothing and bedding, swabs from beer cans, ring-pulls and cigarette stubs, cups and magazines in the hope 'the evidence' would uncover vital new clues.

The police also decided a feminine touch and more precise fingerprinting just might do the trick, and Acting Detective Superintendent Cath Thundercloud, led the re-opened case. She said:

*In Lancashire, we constantly review all our unsolved murder cases,
often undertaking in-depth forensic reviews where modern scientific
techniques can be used. There are many items from the original
investigation which we will be subjecting to modern testing, and
going through original statements to see if there are any inquiries
we can take forward. We didn't have DNA testing at all in 1986,
so we can certainly make advancements. A family liaison officer
has been reappointed and we are keeping Nigel's family up-to-
date. They have been very supportive and are keen for us to do
what we can if it means we may be able to find out who killed
Nigel.*

*Sixteen years ago, details of the investigation were kept on paper
so now officers are delving into the boxes and putting the information
onto the computer and admit its a massive task, which could take
months. In 1986 people were not as open about being gay and may
not have come forward. But now attitudes are much more liberal and
we would like anyone who did know Nigel to contact us.*

Unfortunately, the technological advances still did not help track
down the killer.

However, in August 2004, a new impetus in the effort to catch the
culprits of this horrible crime came, when, nearly eighteen years on,
public attention was again drawn to the case by the BBC's
Crimewatch programme, three years after featuring on a regional TV
reconstruction, and now, with a £5,000 reward being put up by
Crimestoppers to help catch the killer.

On 19 and 20 August 2004, TV crews filmed in a house in
Leyland, Lancashire, recreating the events leading up to the shoe
shop owner's death. The murder featured on the programme on
Tuesday, 21 September, and during the crime busting programme's
reconstruction, details of the complex ligature used to attack and
strangle the shopkeeper were shown.

Another hopeful development had been an anonymous letter
relating to this crime, sent to Southport Police Station, which was
shown for the first time, on *Crimewatch*; though the police had
apparently received it twelve months previously. Some of the
contents of this 'secret note' were made known, in the hope that

its author would make themselves known, as it could be the clue to unlock the mystery. Detective Superintendent Mike Turner said:

We have had the letter for some time now and thanks to information uncovered during the forensic review we now have reason to believe that it could be significant to the inquiry.

Detectives received some leads following this latest new appeal which prompted thirty new calls to the police. The *Crimewatch Update* after the main airing revealed that a good number of the calls were from gay men who had suffered similar attacks. The name of a man in Preston also proved significant to police. Detective Inspector Colin Fish said:

A number of calls provided information about individuals and incidents which supported, and in some cases added to, that already held in the police system. Some calls provided new information about individuals which will require further research prior to being followed up. As the inquiry dates back to 1986 a massive response was not expected, but we are pleased with the number of people who have taken their time to contact us. We do have DNA evidence now so it is easy for us to eliminate innocent people from the investigation. We hope the £5,000 reward from Crimestoppers may encourage someone to make that one important phone call we need to trace, arrest and convict Nigel's killer.

The last piece of the Bostock jigsaw to be picked up came on 1 March 2005, when a man was 'arrested' in connection with the murder - but was released without charge by West Lancashire Police. False alarm. Apparently, the arrest of this forty-seven-year-old Southport man was part of the inquiry trying to get DNA samples from people relevant to the investigation. A police spokeswoman explained:

Not everyone is willing to give a sample, so they are arrested and then given the opportunity to be eliminated from our on-going investigation.

And so, twenty years on, in spite of over 5,000 people being interviewed and the police following more than 2,000 lines of

Another picture of victim Nigel Bostock and a close-up of the stolen Bulova wristwatch. Southport Champion

enquiry, nobody has been found for the murder of Nigel Bostock. The events on that fateful 1986 Christmas party night are still shrouded in mystery.

The chances of catching the killer or killers do seem rather slim but, stranger things have happened.

Anyone with information can ring, in confidence:
Skelmersdale Police 01695 566041
Incident Room 01695 566566
Crimestoppers 0800-555 111

Chapter 8

Sex Demands Row Led to Murder
Sangness Drive, Kew
1992

Kathleen Hobson stabbed her drunken husband, James
McDonald, with two kitchen knives during a late-night
fight at their home, after he demanded unnatural sex.
She was jailed for life – then walked free five years later, on
appeal. Here is a tragic story of a woman who suffered at the
hands of two husbands – bigamy, violence and a death way
out of her control. However, she had also brutally killed
her toddler daughter some eighteen years previously.

Kathleen Hobson's marriage to James McDonald – the man she would later stab to death – began bigamously. The couple wed in July 1990 when, unknown to her, he was still married (which was not dissolved until March 1991). This, her third marriage, was short and stormy, during which they had been physically violent to each other on a number of occasions. Her medical records showed a catalogue of injuries caused from attacks by him. She complained to the police at least four times about his behaviour, but always withdrew the charges.

However, during this roller-coaster marriage thirty-nine-year-old Hobson – her maiden name – had also been violent and attacked thirty-six-year-old Mr McDonald, who was 5ft 5in tall and weighed only eight stones. On one occasion she kicked him in the head and body. It was a case of 'battered husband' syndrome.

On the fateful night of 27 January 1992, Hobson (a clerical officer) and McDonald (a former butcher) had been on a celebratory night out, featuring a romantic candlelit dinner. The

The Sangness Drive home where James McDonald was stabbed to death. Southport Visiter

couple, who were both heavy drinkers, had become reconciled after a separation just a few days before, despite having been married only eighteen months.

She wanted them to talk things over and get back together again – so you could say it was 'Hobson's choice'. The estranged couple spent the afternoon and evening drinking, to celebrate their reunion, his new job and their hopes and plans for a test tube baby. They enjoyed a roast dinner and shared one and a half litre bottles of wine and the best part of a bottle of brandy. When they returned to their home, 26 Sangness Drive – a fairly new house on the Kew estate – they were happy and began dancing to music, smooching, kissing and cuddling to Nat King Cole records.

Hobson's version of events is that her husband began in a gentle loving manner, made love to her, but then changed his sociable attitude a short time later; drunk, he forcefully demanded more sex – but a type she described as 'unnatural'. She then alleged that 'Jimmy' (James McDonald) forced her to have this unnatural (anal) sex, after which she went for a wash, before returned downstairs, in just her nightie. She said:

> *He made a filthy suggestion* [wanted 'unnatural sex' again]. *I went into a cold sweat. I got up and went into the kitchen, maybe to get a drink or something. I must have grabbed hold of the knife. I can't remember.*

Hobson said she kept the knife by her side to stop him approaching her, but he 'just kept coming on strong,' adding:

> *I ran up the stairs, unfortunately the knife was still in my hand. Jimmy managed to grab me down by the ankles. I stumbled and*

grabbed hold of the banister with my left hand and flailed out with my right hand. I didn't want to do anything, it was just automatic. All I can remember is he kept coming on at me and I kept trying to fight him off.

She later told the court that she could not remember anything about the second knife.

In a slightly different version earlier, to the police, she said James had become more and more aggressive and attacked her because she kept refusing his constant sexual demands. As he pursued her around the house she decided to stick up for herself, so grabbed hold of a seven-inch bread knife, initially to arm herself and to scare him away. But still the seedy demands kept coming and the reality of the situation was that she too – not surprisingly – became angry, during what had become a nasty, drunken, late-night fight. His sordid sexual yearnings were repeated over and over, and she later told the court that he became 'vicious and ferocious. It was as if I didn't exist. It was animal instinct. He was basically raping me.'

It was at this point that she lashed out and the blade cut into him. She made a break and fled upstairs, but he chased after her, grabbed hold of her ankles and pulled her back. She swung round and attacked him, stabbing him again, but the knife's handle snapped off. He was now like an injured, outraged bull. She ran back into the kitchen and seized hold of another knife and went back to plunge it into her husband's chest; it was this action that inflicted the fatal stab wound.

Hobson raised the alarm herself just after midnight, ringing emergency services and asking for an ambulance because 'someone was seriously hurt', adding: 'I think I have killed my husband. He is bleeding to death. Please hurry.'

When police and ambulance staff arrived they found all the ground floor rooms looking like a battleground with furniture up-ended and blood everywhere, including the stairs. The victim, James McDonald, was found bare-chested, in a slumped sitting position at the foot of the stairs, on the first landing, bleeding profusely, dying in a pool of blood from six deep knife wounds.

McDonald was rushed to Southport District General Hospital while paramedics struggled in vain to stem the blood from his wounds; doctors fought for two hours to save his life, but it was while he was about to be transferred to Broadgreen Hospital in Liverpool for major chest surgery – which the Southport hospital could not carry out – he died. He was declared dead at about 2.30 am, though some newspaper reports say about 1 am.

Meanwhile, at the southern tip of Kew estate, off Folkestone Road, the Sangness Drive property had been sealed off while police and forensic experts carried out an examination.

The house was heavily bloodstained, with blood covering the walls and carpet and even splattered on a lampshade on the dining room ceiling. The knife – which turned out to be the murder weapon – was discovered by detectives, 'hidden in a drawer containing tea towels'. Another eight-inch carving knife still lay on the floor.

Police officers also found the letter Hobson had written to her husband saying she still loved him and wanted to talk things over:

Before one of us does something silly which we will regret for the rest of our lives.

A post-mortem was carried out and an inquest into McDonald's death opened. The post-mortem exam revealed the cause of death was a stab wound which had penetrated a lung. He had suffered six deep knife wounds, with the injuries including a five-inch slash, and one which went from ear to ear across the back of the neck. The pathologist described the victim as suffering 'from a sustained attack of multiple stab wounds'. Evidence also showed he had been trying to fend off an attack. The summary said that in a sustained assault he had suffered multiple stab wounds, and a fatal blow in the chest which was four inches deep.

The murder incident hit the newspaper stands with headlines such as '*Man dies after stabbing horror,*' and '*Murder Probe: Woman Quizzed.*' The head of CID in Sefton, DS John Corrin had simply told reporters:

Mr McDonald died from stab wounds which had been inflicted with a kitchen knife. A thirty-eight-year-old woman is helping us with our enquiries.

When interviewed, Hobson gave detectives conflicting accounts,

The Pageant, *on the Kew estate, the local pub for Kathleen Hobson and the* *murdered James McDonald.* Author's collection

initially saying she stabbed her husband after he came home drunk and demanded sex, which she refused because she was too tired. She also claimed she had used just the one knife, lashing out purely in self-defence, and that the fatal incident happened on the stairs when her husband demanded unnatural sex.

Neighbours were amazed at James McDonald's death, unaware that behind the net curtains of their respectable, detached home was a cauldron of temper waiting to boil over. Few neighbours knew very much about the couple 'at the end of the road' and it seems they had few friends. The horrific event, however, did not

The interior of The Pageant, *where Hobson had many a row with her ill-fated husband.* Author's collection

come as any great surprise. Sixty-year-old Bill Halsall told the *Southport Visiter* reporter, Paul Smith:

> *No-one really knew the couple well, they kept themselves to themselves, but I always felt there was some abrasiveness there. I would see Mrs Hobson out riding her scooter or going shopping with her husband, but I felt there was a bit of temper. A lot of shouting used to come from the house and the language was a bit colourful, so it didn't come as a 100 per cent surprise.*

Hobson and McDonald were regulars at the fairly recently built *Pageant* pub (opened March 1988), on the nearby Folkestone Road-Ovington Drive corner. On occasions their fiery relationship would bring the place to a standstill. Manager in 1992, Andrew Wilson, said:

> *I would certainly say that they liked a drink. I remember one time when Mr McDonald was having a drink and a suitcase came flying through the door. Mrs Hobson had thrown it, but he just stayed where he was and carried on with his drink. Very soon the two of them were having a set-to with everyone watching.*

Police had to visit the couple's house several times before the murder. Four times officers rushed round after Hobson claimed she had been assaulted by her husband. Three times she withdrew her complaint and on the other occasion police found no evidence for the complaint.

Kathleen Patricia Hobson had been arrested at the crime scene, then officially accused of murdering her husband in the early hours of the Monday morning – and remanded in custody by magistrates in Southport. Defence solicitor Michael Braham made no application for bail and Hobson appeared in court on the Tuesday morning. Reporting restrictions were not lifted. She was remanded in custody for committal on 31 March, and further remanded until April and then held in custody towards committal to Liverpool Crown Court in October, where she pleaded not guilty to murder.

During the trial Hobson admitted stabbing her husband but denied intending to kill him. She also denied the tragic incident had been a raging attack on her husband, saying she had grabbed a knife to scare him away. Hobson denied chasing him around their home and lashing out at him, and denied having used a second knife. Mr Riordan, QC, said:

You were in a rage, you stabbed him from behind, and then, getting another knife you carried on the attack. That is what really happened but you cannot afford to tell the jury that now can you?

Hobson replied: 'That is not how it happened.'

Sentence for her husband's murder had been adjourned to enable the judge to study psychiatric and social inquiry reports, but on Tuesday, 19 October 1992, Hobson was convicted by a jury of murdering her husband and jailed for life. Jailing her, judge Mr Justice Turner remanded her in custody overnight saying the penalty for murder was fixed by law, but he was satisfied that drink had been a major factor in the events that night. He also said he would have to make a recommendation to the Home Secretary about the minimum sentence she serve, taking into account the circumstances of the murder and her past history. It was only after the jury announced their unanimous verdict of 'guilty' that they learned of Kathleen Hobson's violent past. Newspaper headlines included: 'Double killer jailed for life' and 'Murder wife jailed: Mother who had killed her child struck again.'

Defence Counsel, Jonathan Foster, QC, said there had been a

history of drinking and violence but the murder had not been pre-meditated, and that a forensic psychiatrist felt she was not inherently aggressive or violent, adding:

She is distraught at the actions she took that night. This was a loss of self-control by the defendant. She has worked hard all her life, was a sensible woman, and spoken of by the psychiatrist as preoccupied with thoughts of the deceased and suffering a grief reaction.

After the verdict, the court heard that Kathleen Hobson had already served five years for killing her toddler daughter, Deborah, who she strangled with a belt two days before her third birthday, in November 1973. Hobson, then a twenty-year-old, said she had lost her temper when the child threw a tantrum. She wrapped the body of the child (fathered by her first husband) in a sheet, and then drove it to a garage in Runcorn and abandoning it. She then rang the police claiming she had lost her daughter while they were on a shopping expedition and pretended to help in the massive search which was launched. Two days later she confessed and was subsequently jailed for five years for manslaughter by Mold Crown Court.

Kathleen Hobson had become pregnant at sixteen and married the father a year later, but he was violent and she killed their daughter while suffering from chronic depression.

However, events then took a twist. After examining new psychiatric evidence – the Court of Appeal judge quashed Hobson's conviction, in May 1997, and ordered a retrial at Liverpool Crown Court – where she was first convicted. Having been behind bars since the stabbing – serving just over five years of her 'life' sentence – Kathleen Hobson (now forty-four years old) appeared in court on Thursday, 19 June, and a new trial date was fixed for 1 December.

The overturning new evidence indicated that the convicted killer had a defence of either 'diminished responsibility' or 'provocation' – or both. Hobson was said, by her barrister Helena Kennedy, QC. to have: 'matured while in jail and having fortnightly counselling which she planned to continue with such help when outside prison'.

Forty-seven-year-old Helena Kennedy was a prominent barrister who had long campaigned for fairer and better justice for abused women and championed the plight of wives like Kathleen. She argued that Mrs Hobson was suffering from battered woman syndrome at the time of the murder. The high-flying legal eagle had presented programmes on radio and television, and was the creator of the drama series *Blind Justice* in the late 1980s. In the 1990s she wrote articles about legal matters, civil liberties and issues involving women.

Kathleen Hobson was not able to use battered women's syndrome – a sub-division of post traumatic stress disorder – as a defence at her murder trial as it only entered the British classification of mental disease in 1994. She was apparently suffering from low self-esteem and was filled with self-loathing after killing her baby. Her second husband subjected her to humiliating sexual perversions and violence, and then at the hands of her third husband, James McDonald, she was again expected to put up with repeated physical violence.

In court, on Monday, 15 December 1997, the prosecuting counsel Stephen Riordan, QC, who also prosecuted at the original trial, told Mr Justice Smedley: 'As presently advised the Crown wish to proceed to trial. If there is any change in that position we will notify the court as soon as possible.'

He also said that the knives which were exhibits at the first trial had been destroyed and only one had been photographed.

Mr Justice Forbes said anyone listening to the catalogue of violence Kathleen had suffered from an early age at the hands of at least two men, would be filled with profound sadness. He imposed a six-year sentence which, because of the time she had already spent in prison, allowed Hobson's immediate release. He said her plea acknowledged she had killed James McDonald intending to kill or seriously harm him, but she acted as she did because of diminished responsibility and possibly provocation, and that at the time of the killing she had been suffering from what is now recognised as battered wives syndrome.

Mr Forbes said that after hearing from forensic psychiatrist, Dr Gillian Mezey, called by the defence, he was satisfied that Hobson was not a continued danger to the public. Dr Mezey had previously given evidence at the similar high-profile case of Sara Thornton, in May 1996, the first woman to be released after her murder sentence was reduced to manslaughter because of the syndrome. The Warwickshire woman had stabbed her alcoholic policeman husband with a kitchen knife in 1990, as he lay drunk on a sofa.

After the hearing, Hobson declined to talk to the press, but her solicitor, Jim Cullen, of David Phillips & Partners, said: 'I am extremely pleased with the outcome. Since being instructed in 1993 I have always believed that the original verdict should be overturned.'

Women's aid groups and the Probation Service in the North West welcomed the court decision accepted evidence of battered women's syndrome. Eileen Taylor, director of St Helens District Women's Aid, said the evidence was provided by women she saw in the refuge every day, adding: 'We do know that domestic violence syndrome does exist. We are glad the courts are recognising this.' Merseyside Probation Service ran a domestic violence unit which also had an offender programme for men who commit violence. Probation Officer Pat Craven, said:

We are glad the courts are now recognising the extent of the horror of domestic violence on women. It has to start being recognised because it is too serious a problem to ignore. Society at large has been blind to domestic violence.

Ms Craven also said the percentage of cases that reach court are just a fraction of the incidents that occur, and that there were a million reasons for why a woman, who finds herself in a violent situation in the home, does not leave. She concluded:

A woman in Britain dies every three days as a result of domestic violence. The domestic violence problem is absolutely huge and what we are dealing with is just the tip of the iceberg. People say why don't these women just walk out? But for a woman who has been battered it can be very difficult to leave the relationship. Often she is terrified the man will come after her.

However, Dr Sean Stitt, of Liverpool John Moores University, who had researched domestic violence and battered husbands, told the *Liverpool Daily Post* the following day:

I don't believe there is such a thing as battered women's syndrome.

It's just a myth. It is something which is used to excuse women's violence towards males. As a society we have the image that women are not capable of violence. I am very concerned it is being used increasingly to excuse what is violent behaviour by a female.

Dr Stitt said the reason for a woman being violent in certain cases is due to being abused, but that this does not mean it exists as a syndrome. As a reader in community studies, he said we (the public) find it hard to accept women being violent in our society.

The cases of Hobson and Thornton walking free had been widely publicised and rapidly became a cause celebre for women's rights campaigners, giving women's groups hope that another seventy women then serving life sentences for murdering violent partners would be given another hearing.

Chapter 9

An Evil Beast's Masquerade
Stamford Road
1999

No publication about foul deeds in Southport would be complete
without an account of the most horrific crime to hit the resort –
the death of twenty-one-year-old Lynsey Quy, in December 1999,
at the hands of her evil husband, Mitchell. The wicked murder
and gruesome aftermath deeply shocked the seaside town, and
yet the difficult murder investigation was a gripping story that
engrossed people from the start, and was without doubt, the
most detailed and protracted search the town has ever seen.

Lynsey Marie Wilson-Quy, a petite, freckle-faced young woman, saw her parents for the last time on 10 December 1998; she then mysteriously vanished, never to be seen again. The chilling disappearance of Lynsey was the talk of the town and unfound rumours of her whereabouts were constantly rife. The pages of the local newspapers and the region's airwaves were dominated at the end of the decade by the mystery.

Her husband, Mitchell, claimed Lynsey had walked out on Christmas Day 1998, abandoning her two children Robyn, five, and Jack, three, for another man. He kept up this charade by insisting Lynsey had left him and the children, and even appeared on television appealing for

Lynsey Marie Wilson-Quy. The Wilson family

Lynsey's mum and dad, Peter and Linda Wilson. Southport Champion

Lynsey with Jack, the eldest of her two children. The Wilson family

Pure Evil – murderer Mitchell Quy. Author's collection

her to come home – appearing to be a loving husband and doting father.

But the brutal truth was he had strangled his wife and kept her body in a bedroom, then the loft of their home, 22 Stamford Road, while he worked out his next move. Family life continued as normal.

'Missing Person' posters were put up around Southport, but twenty-four-year-old Quy claimed he had seen his 5ft 1in tall wife three times, saying he spotted her being driven in a black Mercedes, and in the King Street indoor market. He also said that Lynsey, who had long, straight, dark brown hair, was sporting a new hairstyle and wearing new clothes.

Mitchell Quy had not reported his wife as missing, insisting she 'ran off with another fella'. Concern was only raised fifty-three days later, in February, when police were called in by staff at a nursery when little Robyn failed to turn up. But by then Quy had enlisted the help of his twenty-two-year-old brother, Elliott, to dispose of Lynsey's body. Mitchell Quy was jailed for life in January 2001 after pleading guilty to her murder.

Lynsey was born in Ormskirk on 5 September 1977, the fourth of six children and father Peter Wilson's first and only daughter. Brought up in Skelmersdale until she was four-years-old, the quiet and shy Shoreside Primary School pupil, was a caring, happy, popular and hardworking Ainsdale High schoolgirl. As a young woman she was smart, attractive, very lively, friendly, outspoken and above all devoted to her children.

Lynsey became pregnant at sixteen in February 1995, with her first serious boyfriend, got engaged, but broke it off. Living alone in Albany Road with a five-month-old baby, and on the rebound, Lynsey's enigmatic smile captivated Mitchell Quy, and after a five-week whirlwind romance married the nineteen-year-old casino croupier on 1 August 1995, at Southport Town Hall. Quy – who

MERSEYSIDE POLICE

MISSING

DO YOU KNOW THIS WOMAN ?

Lyndsey-Wilson <u>Quy</u>

(Age 22 years)

Lyndsey is white, 5 ft 1˝ tall, of Slim build

British, with long brown/black hair,

brown/green eyes,

Freckles & a small dark spot on her right cheek

IF YOU HAVE ANY INFORMATION

PLEASE CONTACT

SOUTHPORT POLICE STATION ON 0151-777 3551 / 3535

OR CRIMESTOPPERS 0800 555111

Southport Police's 'Missing' Poster. Merseyside Police

was born in Chelmsford, Essex, on 13 February 1975 – had no family at the wedding, except his younger brother, Elliott.

But it was a tempestuous marriage; disputes were frequent and he often hit her. During October 1996 she terminated her pregnancy after having serious doubts about their marriage lasting. He never forgave her and carried on doing what he had always done, slept around. Lynsey then started divorce proceedings, after obtaining a restraining order on Quy.

In April 1997 she took him back, and quickly fell pregnant, but a month later he snapped again and wrecked their small rented flat at 111 Boundary Street, smashing every item and hurling the television through the window. Lynsey's sister warned her: 'One day he will kill you.'

Quy was placed on probation, but there was a second incident when he smashed up the house, systematically throwing garden rockery stones through windows. All the while he said nothing. Then he jumped up and down on his car.

However, they stayed together and Jack was born in the October, but they split up again in the April after more beatings, and then, in the summer of 1998 he raped her on the floor in the house in front of the children. She became so scared of him that she obtained another injunction, and was given a personal attack alarm by the Police Domestic Violence Unit.

Lynsey, who had spent all her life in the seaside resort, eventually began to make a new life for herself after help to set up a home, which she practically turned into a nursery.

But, being lonely, she made a terrible mistake, in October 1998, when she got back with 'Mitch' after he used Jack's first birthday as an excuse to wheedle his way back into her affections – with a bunch of flowers. She very soon regretted it, but unfortunately it was a mistake that would cost her life. Quy's tantrums escalated. One day Lynsey handed her step-sister Paula a note, pretending it was a new telephone number, but it said: 'Please Help Me.'

In November 1998, she discovered her husband had (again) stolen her £84 benefits giro cheque. Being meticulous about keeping her books straight, and with Christmas coming, she confronted her wayward husband, which caused another row.

On 15 December, Lynsey arranged to see a solicitor to finalise divorce proceedings, to get Quy out of her home for good, but the former *Dungeon* nightclub barmaid never made it. In the heat of a furious all-day long argument, she let it slip and told him he would not see the children again. Quy, who had tried to kill himself after a previous threat of divorce, began to renew his threat, but snapped into a furious rage – in his words, 'over-reacted' and 'just lost it'. Unable to take this final rejection, he killed his wife in the early hours of 16 December, while the children slept.

High on cannabis and after drinking five cans of Guinness, Lynsey's violent husband grabbed her neck, forced her to the lounge floor and slowly strangled her with his bare hands. He held her face down for twenty minutes, and squeezed and squeezed. From the side he saw a single tear roll down one of her cheeks, when there was no life left in her body. The evil beast had finally snapped, because his wife wanted to end their stormy, violent life together.

The police believed that moments later he carried out a kind of ritualistic stabbing, after a pathologist found stab wounds on Lynsey's body, which they couldn't explain. Quy said he had blanked out the episode. In court he said that after throttling his wife of three years, he tried to resuscitate her and considered contacting the emergency services.

Lynsey's limp body was then carried and dragged upstairs and put into bed, and left there for three days while he wondered what to do. Family life continued as if nothing had happened.

The day after, Quy took the children to his younger brother's house, and calmly confessed to the murder, persuading him to help. Reluctantly, Elliott did. They transferred the body to Mitchell's loft. Wrapped tightly in bed linen, it stayed hidden for five days – while Mitchell resumed sleeping in the matrimonial bed.

From there the murder took a more sinister twist.

Elliott, a handyman, of Church Street, agreed to assist Mitchell with the gruesome task of cutting and chopping up poor Lynsey's body. With access to a variety of tools, Elliott chose a high-tensile

Blood-brothers, Elliott (left) and Mitchell Quy. The Wilson family

hacksaw with double-edged teeth, a pruning saw, Stanley (carpet) knife, screwdriver, and a claw hammer 'for the job'.

The brothers brought Lynsey's body down from the roof space, put her in the bath and then set about dismembering it – while the two children lay asleep in the next room. The stench was so bad they had to seal the door frame with masking tape to prevent the odour seeping out, putting tea towels, smeared with toothpaste, over their faces to block the smell.

Mitchell first severed the head and hands, and then cut the torso at the waist, legs and arms. Elliott told detectives, quite matter of factually, that Mitchell – who did the majority of the cutting – handed him each body piece which he put in a bag. The dismembering process took two days and then the evil blood brothers were faced with the question of what to do next.

Not only was Lynsey killed, but the evil Birkdale beast bequeathed one last indignity on her – by allowing his brother to put her decapitated head and hands into a bin bag and left out with the refuge collection. To make identification of the remains more difficult, Elliott disposed of them on his way home, dumping them amongst rubbish bags outside a Birkdale grocery shop. They were never recovered.

Mitchell wrapped his wife's arms and legs tightly in black plastic bin liners, placed them in a rucksack, and the next day set off into the town centre with it on his back. One-year-old Jack was in the pram while three-year-old Robyn in tow walked alongside her dad, clutching his hand. As they strolled along Mitchell calmly hid 'the parcels' in shallow graves. Little Robyn later recalled him 'throwing parcels away'. The two brothers had a pact that they would not tell each other where they had put the parts.

It wasn't until 5 February 1999, that Social Services became concerned for Lynsey's welfare and reported the mother-of-two as missing, after they had been contacted by Bury Road pre-school nursery.

Police visited the couple's Birkdale home, but Lynsey's unemployed husband proclaimed she had come home at 7 am, 'off her face' (drunk) after a Christmas Eve night out with a friend. Then, a few hours later simply 'upped and left' with a suitcase of clothes at 2 pm on Christmas Day, without saying goodbye to her children, leaving their presents unopened.

Quy hadn't said anything because 'she had run off with another fella,' and her parents were giving the couple space to sort out their marriage, although Mitchell was disliked.

An intensive missing person investigation was launched, and the CID officers searched the former barmaid's home – as a routine procedure – and interviewed neighbours, taxi-drivers, local organizations and friends.

From the start Southport Police had the former croupier down as their prime suspect. His body language and facial expressions gave him away, but without a body it was almost an impossible task for the police. But in Quy's own televised words 'eventually everyone will find out the truth'. The police said: 'When we've got a body, we've got our man!'

The Wilsons might not have been a very close-knit family, but Quy left them guilt-ridden, thinking they could or should have done something to prevent the tragedy.

Mitchell Quy spoke at a news conference on Wednesday, 17 February, pretending to appeal for his wife to come home, and footage was shown on regional and national television. He claimed she had returned home to pick up some clothes, but he did not see her, but no money had been withdrawn from her bank account.

Lynsey's parents, forty-nine-year-old Linda Wilson and her ex-husband forty-eight-year-old Peter, made an emotional appeal on GMTV. They later added:

> We are worried sick, Lynsey would never leave the children, and she was always with them and adores them. We are out of our minds with worry. Every minute she is missing our fears for her safety are growing. This is so out of character. Lynsey was not happy at home and she was having trouble in her relationship with Mitch. So we decided to leave them alone to sort it out. We don't think that she would walk away and leave the children, especially on Christmas Day.

One of Lynsey's friends summed up the situation:

> If she decided to leave she would have taken the children. I hope she has gone off with someone, but deep down I feel that something awful could have happened.

Despite a huge police search no leads were established, so detectives turned to technology – the computerized missing person's database CATCHEM (Central Analytical Team Collating Homicide Expertise and Management).

Detectives had searched the couple's home on three occasions – and even brought in an X-ray machine; but despite electronically scanning the floorboards and back garden, no body emerged. Stories of a foreign trip were also dismissed, as she had never been

Mitchell Quy calmly stands aside, in June 1999, as police search his home for clues.
Daily Post

further than Blackpool on holiday and didn't even possess a passport.

The mystery of Lynsey's disappearance deepened, and speculation was fuelled when her estranged husband admitted their three-year marriage had deteriorated, and become 'a nightmare'. But Quy – who was Lynsey's second husband – denied any foul deed:

There was never any trust – we got married too soon. I didn't expect

*her to leave the kids. I thought she was going for a couple of weeks on
her own and then come back. When I walk down the street or in shops
I notice people talking, or have said things, but I am obviously going
to get that. Overall, people have been very supportive.*

Mrs Wilson recalled her attractive, 'bubbly' and 'big hearted'
daughter, who was particularly close to her father, as a person who
could storm off in a rage and would not be seen for weeks, but would
then walk miles to deliver you a birthday present. She added:

*It's hard to think that your daughter has been murdered. It took some
time before I was convinced, but her father knew immediately that she
was dead. I want to find my daughter to lay her to rest and I want
the person responsible to be caught.*

As fears for the young mum grew, the investigation was intensified in
March, when a fifteen-strong specialist team was brought in to
physically search marshland surrounding Lynsey's Birkdale home,
including (Fine) Jane's Brook. Mechanical diggers unearthed fields in
response to aerial photographs the police helicopter took with infra-
red cameras. Frogmen meticulously probed and dredged ditches and
sewers and sniffer dogs and mounted police scoured other areas. But
still, nothing! Meanwhile, the *Champion* newspaper distributed 5,000
'missing person' leaflets in the Birkdale and Ainsdale area.

All the while, Mitchell Quy continued to protest his innocence,
and even complained that he was being victimized.

The distraught family shared their photographs of Lynsey with
the *Southport Visiter* and *Southport Champion* newspapers, hoping
the selected album snaps would prompt Lynsey to get in touch.
Anxiously waiting her father said:

*We just don't know what to do with ourselves. It's hard work trying
to pull everyone together with the constant worry of where she may
be. We're all starting to fear the worst, but will never give up hope; this
is a living nightmare and such a horrible situation to be in – as far
as we're concerned no news is not good news.*

Lynsey's thirty-year-old step-sister, Paula Houghton, of
Churchtown, added:

Lynsey is a loving mother, a caring sister and a devoted daughter, and

22 Stamford Road, where Lynsey Quy was butchered. Wilson family

she would have never left the children. Her disappearance has brought the family closer together, although sadly it's also ripped us apart.

In March the Merseyside Scientific Support Department returned to the semi-detached property and spent five hours at the former Stanley Casino croupier's home carrying out 'a routine forensic examination', removing four bags of Lynsey's clothing, toiletries and personal items for analysis. The police said:

We will continue the search for Lynsey. She is still missing from home and there are all sorts of avenues we have to explore yet. If members of the public have phoned in and mentioned specific locations we'll act upon them. All the searches are logical and routine steps – we started at the home, like any missing persons inquiry. Rumours and innuendo are rife throughout Southport at the moment, but we must deal with evidence and hard facts. We are urging people to stop speculating on unfound rumours, as this is very traumatic and upsetting for the family and friends.

The inquiry took a twist when Quy was arrested at his home at 9.45 am on Monday, 12 April, on 'suspicion of murder', as well as old charges of assault and criminal damage incidents at the couple's former home in Boundary Street. He was questioned at great length, not charged with murder, but bailed to face three complicated offences of incitement to commit grievous bodily harm to Lynsey back in February 1997. During this time the children were looked after by the Wilson family, who had not seen them since Lynsey's disappearance.

In a desperate bid, Peter Wilson donned a borrowed wet suit, armed himself with ropes, a stick and a hook, and for four months physically combed numerous dirty, smelly waterways, mosses and scrubland throughout the district, hoping to find some clues – or worse, Lynsey's body. He was often joined by other family members. The searches came after a drawing from a London psychic illustrated Lynsey's body was submerged in water by a rock and electricity pylon. The frustrated parents even sought help from the world famous psychic Uri Geller, who also pinpointed 'a burial site' but that was a negative.

However, chilling words uttered by a psychic from Manchester will haunt Peter Wilson forever. She claimed that Lynsey's spirit spoke to her during a reading. The amazing statement was:

He cut me up, he cut me up, he put me in a wheelie bin. I can't feel anything from the waist down. I feel a terrible pain in my head.

A study by crime specialists and civil engineers in May, ruled out upsetting rumours that Lynsey was buried underneath Southport's new £5m white-knuckle ride, the Traumatizer, at Pleasureland. But the *Daily Sport* published an insensitive article headlined: 'Wife is Buried Under Big Dipper', which spouted unfounded speculation that Lynsey was buried deep in the rollercoaster's foundations. Peter Wilson was furious as well as very upset, and contacted the Press Complaints Commission in disgust at the appalling sensationalism.

As Lynsey's disappearance hit the 150th day, GBH charges against Quy were dropped by the Crown Prosecution Service, but the egotistical Quy again taunted the police by threatening to sue them for 'substantial' damages (roughly £15,000), for 'wrongful arrest' and for repeatedly questioning him. Quy said the charges 'were a pathetic joke'.

The six-month mystery took a twist when it was upgraded to a murder investigation, making Mitchell Quy an official suspect – prompted due to the lack of independent sightings of Lynsey – and Detective Superintendent Geoff Sloan took over the case and re-examined every aspect of the investigation, saying:

DS Geoff Sloan who led the murder hunt. Southport Champion

Despite extensive police inquiries, there is no proof that she is still alive. In fact, we are now assuming she is dead and has been murdered. Given the nature and character of the girl, I thought it would be inconceivable that she would have abandoned her children on that special day.

Could modern science solve Lynsey's murder? Specially-trained police officers and military-trained experts returned to the Stamford Road house, on Tuesday, 15 June, with a sophisticated, ultra-sensitive scanner, which could trace bodies. They spent two days x-raying the garden and patio, but no results were gleaned.

A new twenty-two-strong police search team trawled wasteland off Bentham's Way, and found a bundle of women's clothing, which were assessed by an entomologist. The clothes were the right size and style, and included a metal medallion, like a St Christopher, which was similar to one Peter Wilson used to have. But, it was a false alarm. Later, it was suggested Quy had planted these.

Lynsey's father then received a royal letter from the Queen expressing her sympathy, but in July, Lynsey's unimpressed dad blasted a Granada TV *Crimefile* reconstruction as 'disgusting' and said he was 'horrified' that it 'didn't show their daughter how she really was'.

Mitchell Quy was again in court, on Wednesday, 14 July, pleading guilty to a total of seven charges of forgery and deception/fraud, after dishonestly claiming over £420 of DSS Income Support in his wife's name, and making two cheques payable to himself, forging Lynsey's name, amounting to £200. Lynsey's family protested outside court with placards, and wore badges bearing Lynsey's face, trying to persuade him to say where Lynsey was. On 5 August he was sentenced to 120 hours community service, but later made an astonishing attack on the police, saying:

They are making me out to be some sort of psychopath. They have searched my house five times now, but I've done nothing wrong. They are just looking for an easy conviction. It's a nightmare, I want a public apology. The police want to get me, I know, but I just plod on and laugh at their efforts. When I was arrested they kept asking me where she was, where I'd put her, but I've got nothing to hide. They keep applying pressure expecting me to break, but I just snapped back – 'No comment.'

Mitchell Quy's face was that of a killer, one that gave him away every time the brazen, cold-hearted man opened his mouth. For eighteen

Happy families. Lynsey and Mitchell with their children visiting friends in the resort.
The Wilson family

months he arrogantly denied his guilt; he lied to the police, the press, his family and friends. He thought he had got away with murder with his cruel campaign, keeping up the image of an abandoned father, hoping for public sympathy, and callously lying that Lynsey was still alive. It was just one lie after the other for this misguided individual, but his confidence was growing, and in what had become a serious cat-and-mouse game, Quy even goaded DS Sloan by sending him a hair colouring kit – to rid him of the grey hairs the case was giving him.

But it was all too much for Lynsey's exhausted family. After searching watercourses in Burscough and Lathom, they stopped their personal searches, because it was too upsetting. Sadness then surrounded Robyn's fourth birthday; this was the milestone that Quy said he would have to tell Robyn that 'mummy isn't coming back – because she's with someone else'.

Quy became a 'killer on the couch' in front of millions of viewers, when he appeared live on ITV's *This Morning* programme, with celebrity husband and wife presenters Richard Madeley and Judy Finnegan. Richard asked him point-blank: 'Did you kill your wife?' Quy looked him straight in the eye, grinned and curtly replied: 'No, I didn't.' A few weeks later, and constantly chewing gum, he again lied his way through a live interview, on *Granada Tonight*, with presenter Mark Owen.

Early in the December, someone took a pot shot at Quy's house, when a pellet pierced his front room window. Then, for the fifth time, he reappeared in court for failing to carry out his community service orders. He then began doing five hours every Monday in a charity shop.

Since Lynsey went missing Quy had received several threatening telephone calls. One message, in a chilling voice – which Quy called 'pathetic and small-minded' said:

> *Your conscience must be burning inside you with what you have done to that poor girl. You're an animal, a beast – you're the devil. Your conscience will destroy you. If that doesn't we will.*

Despite saying he was staying out of the press, Quy pledged to personally take the search Europe-wide in the New Year, and Granada TV's *Real Life* producers began making an hour-long documentary about Lynsey's disappearance, with cameras following Quy's every move.

A year on, Mitchell Quy had become the most recognized man in Southport, but the inquiry appeared to have stalled. Despite thousands of police man-hours and extensive excavations, there was still no clue to Lynsey's whereabouts. But, the enquiries went on, unrelented.

Developments finally came. DS Sloan took assertive action. A fleet of unmarked police cars and a transit van full of officers swooped on Stamford Road to arrest Mitchell Quy just before 8 am on Wednesday, 7 June 2000, on suspicion of murder. Quy's arrest had been inevitable – it was just a matter of time! The 'cool campaigner' said his situation was like a bad dream, it was about to be turned into a nightmare! But no-one knew just what horror lay in store, and of the dramatic and ultimately gruesome events which would unfold.

Three officers took Quy, while the children left with a liaison officer to spend the night with their grandparents; Quy's fifty-two-year-old father, Michael, had also been picked up some ten miles away at his modern detached home in Briars Lane, Lathom, about half-an-hour earlier. The third Quy, brother Elliott, was taken into custody the following night and charged with the conspiracy and, assisting an offender in the disposal of Mrs Quy.

For thirty-six hours – their deadline for detainment being extended – Mitchell Quy used his 'Rights to Silence' card and simply kept saying 'no comment,' but detectives had an ace up their sleeve – a radical new interview technique, a fresh tactic. A behavioural expert re-analysed all Quy's responses, even media interviews. Quy had never wavered from his well-rehearsed script, so had to be disjointed. An unfamiliar re-interview venue was used, Copy Lane, Liverpool, and he was taken there in a police van, not a comfy unmarked car. All this manipulation turned the tables, and each new stern question was like a body blow. Detectives then watched as he recoiled, broke down, and then they couldn't shut him up. Before the decision to formally charge him with murder, he poured out his disgusting confession. Quy had finally cracked. The devious killer's solicitor passed a handwritten note to the custody officer from his client, saying:

The person who conspired with me in Lynsey's death was Elliott. My father had nothing to do with it. He does not know what happened.

This murder case, which had been the subject of intense public debate for so long, had taken a gruesome twist. By the time detectives got back to Quy, he hadn't just spelt it out, he had drawn

One of the horror scenes where parts of Lynsey Quy's body were found. Southport Champion

them a picture. It was a scribbled diagram of where 'all the body parts were' – he had systematically and callously dismembered his wife.

An unshaven Mitchell Quy appeared at Southport Magistrates Court on Friday, 9 June, charged with murder and he and his father were also both charged with conspiracy to pervert the course of justice, by pretending she was still alive.

On Saturday, 10 June, the tragic news was given to the devastated parents of missing Lynsey that her severed body had been found, just after 8 pm the previous night, and eighteen months of fears were realized.

After his brief court appearance, Quy took the police on a horrific tour to various Southport locations where Lynsey's mutilated body had been dumped. The notorious publicity seeker had the gall to try and joke with officers at the grim scenes where the broken-up body lay, asking if the press were following and the cameras rolling.

The grim discovery of a severed right leg, and a left leg the following day, was made in undergrowth on the railway embankment at the end of Banastre Road, half-a-mile from Lynsey's home. Another find, her headless torso (which Quy described as 'the carcass') and arms without hands, was by Princes Park and zoo, behind Pleasureland's go-kart track. Police frogmen then searched under a busy pedestrian bridge in Marine Lake looking for a knife, unsuccessfully. Southport

Peter Wilson jnr (24), who committed suicide following the death of his beloved sister. The Wilson family

residents were deeply shocked by the grisly week-long search for body parts, although it didn't stop crowds gathering to watch. Lynsey's father said:

> *This is beyond belief – more horrendous than we ever thought it would be. Nobody ever expects to hear their daughter has been found in bits all over Southport. This has been a horror from the start to the finish. The family is gutted and the thought of burying her like she is, is just horrific. To kill someone is one thing but to actually chop someone up is just unforgivable. I can't see the point of what has happened, it's pure evil.*

Peter Wilson later praised the police for their investigation and determination throughout the case, and said the children had been told 'their mummy has died and gone to heaven'. He then said a big thank you to the many well-wishers who left cards and floral tributes outside Lindsey's home. A pink teddy was tied to the door, with a card attached reading:

> *Sleep tight mummy. Will miss you always. Love you loads, Robyn and Jack.*

Peter adding:

> *I feel hatred towards Mitchell. I was convinced from day one he had murdered her and it has been difficult to cope because of that. At the*

beginning I pestered him and asked where Lynsey's body was and he used to say 'I don't know where she is,' then I got letters from his solicitors.

But it was the action of numerous on-lookers, 'ghoulish spectators,' that caught the attention of the *Southport Visiter*. At one point more than 100 people watched the police divers. In its editorial *Our View*, human nature and morbid curiosity was highlighted, as many bought ice creams and watched in fascination in baking temperatures. The column exclaimed: 'What can be made of the behavior of two people who brought along deckchairs to sit and watch the search for the unfortunate mother's remains?'

The police called off their search for the remains of butchered Lynsey, due to the sheer scale of the task. It would have involved 200,000 tonnes of household and clinical waste and eight million bin bags, which would have taken an estimated three years to search.

On remand at Walton Prison, handcuffed Quy appeared before magistrates on Friday, 17 June, for a brief committal hearing, with a strong police presence at the Albert Road court. Then there were angry scenes outside the packed Southport Magistrates' Court on Friday, 7 July, after the appearance of the three Quys, together for the first time, when the case was adjourned to allow the defence to examine committal papers amounting to 1,500 pages. A number of friends and family were asked to remove badges with pictures of Lynsey on.

A brief inquest into Lynsey's death, by Sefton's deputy coroner Alfred Cook, was held at the end of July, to establish that blood samples from her parents, using DNA profile evidence, matched the dismembered body parts belonging to their daughter. After three adjournments, how Lynsey was actually killed still remained a mystery, as the earlier post-mortem was inconclusive.

United in grief, family and friends said a final farewell to Lynsey, with two emotionally-charged services, on Monday, 14 August. As the long funeral cortege, with police escort, made its way from Lynsey's childhood home in Sussex Road to a private funeral at Southport Crematorium (service by the Reverend Ian

Stockley), dozens of residents lined the streets. The coffin was flanked by poignant floral tributes of white carnations spelling out *Lynsey* and *Mummy*, topped with a single red rose symbolizing a young life tragically cut short. Another poignant moment was the floral card from Lynsey's parents which symbolically used her maiden name of Wilson, as if to reclaim their daughter for her birth family.

Some 300 people, including detectives from the investigation, then attended Holy Trinity church for a memorial and thanksgiving service, led by the Reverend Rod Garner, where mourners were visibly moved by tributes from Lynsey's closest friends recalling her smile, friendship, love and support. The service, which brought out the best in a community, was a celebration of Lynsey's life. For her family, who had maintained extraordinary composure since she disappeared, it was one of their hardest days, but through their tears they showed enormous dignity. Two photographs of a smiling Lynsey, her dark hair flowing, were placed at the front of the church, with a sea of white lilies at the base of the altar. *All Things Bright and Beautiful* and *Morning Has Broken* were sung, and mourners left the church to *The Wind Beneath My Wings*. Lynsey's ashes were placed in two urns, one to be scattered in Cornwall where she had planned to start a new life, the other placed by her great grandmother's grave at Duke Street Cemetery.

Meanwhile, a row erupted over a novel, *The Singing Dead*, by Ron Ellis, about a massive police hunt for a missing young mum-of-two in Southport who mysteriously walks out on her husband, and tells how the Marine Lake and Traumatiser are dug up – but his story ends with her returning from Spain. Peter Wilson accused the criminal scribe of 'an insensitive reference to his daughter's death,' but the author denied it was based on murdered Lynsey.

During festive time 2000, generous Southport residents bought presents for Lynsey's children – who had been looked after by the Wilson family since the summer – donated as gifts via the Salvation Army, to help them enjoy a better Christmas.

Lynsey's parents had divorced ten years previously, but got back

Happier days – the wedding of Lynsey Wilson to Mitchell Quy. Elliott Quy is centre, back row. The Wilson family

together again for the sake of the children. On 19 January 2000, they applied to become the legal guardians of six-year-old Robyn – who attended the funeral services – and three-year-old Jack.

The 'blood brothers' were in court on 18 September, when Mitchell pleaded not guilty to murder, but admitted manslaughter. His lawyer, Ian Harris, said the issue to be decided by the jury was diminished responsibility and/or provocation. Elliott admitted helping to dispose of his sister-in-law's body. They were remanded until 15 January 2001. Surprisingly, the charge against Michael Anthony Quy, was dropped due to lack of evidence.

The 15 January trial was expected to last three weeks, but it was completed within a day. Mitchell Quy came before a jury at Liverpool Crown Court on Tuesday, 16 January 2001. He had earlier pleaded not guilty to murder, but in a dramatic twist, late on, he changed his mind. Dressed in a dark blue double-breasted suit, dark blue shirt and patterned tie, Quy spoke only to confirm his name and plead guilty to the murder charge – which brought gasps of relief from the packed public gallery, but no reaction at all from the defendant.

Andrew Edis, prosecuting, told the courtroom of the stormy and often violent marriage that ended in murder. The pair had separated on more than one occasion and Lynsey had started divorce proceedings, but gone back to him.

Lynsey's family were in the packed courtroom and applauded as the judge sentenced Mitchell, who stood stony-faced throughout the hour-long session. After putting the Wilsons through nearly 400 days of unimaginable anguish, trial judge, Mr Justice Brian Leveson told Quy that his innocence campaign was a 'deceit of breathtaking cynicism', describing him as 'evil' for the way he made the children believe their mother had abandoned them.

Later, the judge praised the police and complimented the officer in charge of the case, Detective Chief Superintendent Geoff Sloan and his team, including Detective Sergeant Mark Dale and Detective Constable Keith Parkinson, Nick Hope and Peter Hough, as well as Alistair Jones and Nyree Kerr for their roles. He added:

Many investigations require very great effort. This was clearly one, and you deserve the highest commendation. Please ensure my remarks are past on to the Chief Constable.

Mitchell Quy was sentenced to life in prison for murdering his wife on 16 December 1998. He showed no emotion as he was led away to jail. David Turner, QC, defending, had told the court that it was the fear of losing his children which motivated Quy to continue lying.

But that question comes begging again – just how long is life? It is frightening to think that someone described as 'just pure evil' could spend anything less than the rest of their life behind bars. No guidelines over the length of the sentence was given, but later, in June 2001, it was announced that Quy must serve at least seventeen years before being eligible for parole. That is the minimum time, so he could remain behind bars much longer.

In January 2001, Lynsey's dad responded with disgust at Mitchell Quy's hopes of being reunited with his children when he is released from prison, adding: 'Mitchell has as much chance of seeing the children again as Lynsey.'

Elliott James Quy, of Church Street, received seven years for helping to dispose of the body and making false statements to conceal the truth – which was done out of 'sheer blind loyalty'. But Peter Wilson said the sentence was not long enough, and described how Lynsey used to care for her brother-in-law by cooking him meals, including Christmas dinner in 1997 when he was on his own in a bedsit, and she washed his clothes.

But shocking news came in February 2005 when Elliott was released early on licence, after serving just four years. Peter Wilson said: 'It's a disgrace that this animal can be let out, he should serve ten years – he played as much a part in Lynsey's murder as Mitchell.'

It was a case that shocked Southport. Mitchell Quy had been asked directly, and in all seriousness, on television's *Prime Suspect* – 'Did you kill Lynsey?' He replied:

I'm not gonna answer that. Wait and find out. One day everyone will know the truth, won't they.

The Lynsey Quy Fund was set up by local resident Wendy Miller, to raise the money to send the two children on a holiday-of-a-lifetime, and various benefit nights were organized.

In March 2001, there was a bizarre claim that Mitchell Quy had married a twenty-nine-year-old woman who visited the convicted killer at Altcourse Prison. Following two suicide attempts he was transferred to Swaleside Prison, Kent.

Sadly, the consequences of Mitchell Quy's evil actions resulted in further heartache, when Lynsey's twenty-four-year-old brother,

Peter, hanged himself on Monday, 23 April 2001, at the family home in Sussex Road. The burden of being the person who introduced Lynsey to Quy and the murderous loss of his sister was too heavy for Peter, although nobody blamed him. Lynsey's death had deeply affected him. He was found at 8 pm by his father. His funeral took place on Wednesday, 2 May – two days after what would have been his twenty-fifth birthday.

Peter Wilson, in Ainsdale Lake, during one of his many searches for his 'missing' daughter. The Wilson family

Chapter 10

Notorious Hard-Men in Double Horror Attack
Derby Road
2002

Southport residents woke up one warm, summer morning in June 2002, to one of the most horrific murders the town has ever witnessed, committed by two notorious 'hard-men'. Jealousy was the only motive for the vicious killing of two men bludgeoned in a savage and frenzied attack with a mettal baseball bat, at a town centre flat. The victims pleaded for mercy, but none was given by the cold-hearted killers, and the double murder trial was to blow the top off the secrecy which surrounds Southport's drugs underworld.

This chilling murder case was certainly one of Southport's most gruesome foul deeds. Paul Hagan and Francis Perry's death did not come quick, the injuries they received are usually only sustained in the worst possible motorcycle crashes. There was blood everywhere; the horrendous and frenzied attacks had gone on for some considerable time. One of the victims of the prolonged battering had a hinge fracture of the skull, where it actually came apart.

This was the first – and so-far only – double murder in the seaside resort's history. The last multiple murderer was Dr Clements, fifty-five years previously, who grabbed the headlines in 1947 for single-handedly poisoning his wives (Chapter 2), but this incident was during a single event, by two people.

The timeline of events began on the morning of Tuesday, 18

Paul Hagan (left) and Francis Perry, murdered by two vicious Southport bouncers while visiting friends in the resort. Southport Champion

June, when Paul and Francis came to Southport. Despite coming from Huyton, they were quite well known here. Thirty-six-year-old Paul Hagan, of Darwick Drive, was about to become a father for the fourth time as his partner was five months pregnant, and forty-year-old Francis Perry, of Reeds Road, known fondly as 'Buddy,' was described as a kind, very funny man. The two men worked together as roofers.

Two days before the killings the victims had attended the funeral of a friend in Huyton where they met fifty-two-year-old James ('Jimmy') MacElhinney – a mutual friend. The next day the three met up again and visited pubs in Huyton, before driving to Southport, intending to stay the night at Mr MacElhinney's flat, in Derby Road, a converted Victorian house facing the then new Asda superstore.

In the late afternoon and evening the trio enjoyed visiting town centre pubs, meeting friends, drinking at various bars and nightclubs. The men became separated from the flat's occupant, and ended up in the *West End Club* and then *Waverley's*, on Waverley Street, off Lord Street, about 12:30 pm, where their two killers were also drinking. One of them, Raffaele Esposito, met Hagan and

Raffaele Esposito, who flew into a jealous rage, and committed murder. Southport Visiter

Perry who were by now fairly drunk but still wanted to carry on drinking; Esposito took him along with his sister and girlfriend, both in their late teens. So, the two men conversed with these two females, Giustina Esposito and Melissa Thompson.

One of the girls also lived in the same block of flats as Jimmy – where the victims would later be found – and the same house where Esposito had an adjacent flat.

Inside the *West End Club*, Esposito became angry, because he believed that Paul and Francis had been 'acting inappropriately' by being 'over-familiar' with the two young women. He then summoned his friend Sean Jackman to help him 'sort them out'.

The defendants were mates who occasionally worked together. Esposito was the licensee of *Bar Farino's* and part-time doorman. Jackman worked at various Southport venues, including the *West End Club*. He had been a licensee in the town for almost four years.

Meanwhile, Giustina left the club and sometime later Melissa left with the two victims to go back to Jimmy's Derby Road flat. All appeared to get on perfectly well. Both originally from Ormskirk, eighteen-year-old Melissa and seventeen-year-old Guistina, walked back to the house with the victims, and left Hagan and Perry to wait in the flat for their friend 'Mac'.

Just before 2 am Giustina spoke briefly to her brother by mobile 'phone – obviously upset -and about that time, he and Jackman left the club. Half an hour later Esposito rang another bouncer, Joseph Sammon to join his 'troops' and a further half an hour later the torment began.

Paul Hagan and Francis Perry were brutally murdered in the early hours of Wednesday morning, between 2 am and 4 am, following a protracted beating of considerable savagery. The heartless murderers showed no mercy to the dying men; as they delivered the bloody blows the victims were 'begging for their lives' as the evil doormen clubbed them to death in a drugs and alcohol fuelled frenzy. The cold-blooded killers were high on cocaine. It was not a sudden loss of temper, the killings were senseless and deliberate, a tragic waste of life. It was a planned ambush.

A gruesome picture emerged of the brutal and sustained attack, with the horrendous injuries being inflicted by a baseball bat, calor gas bottle, a bread knife, golf club, fists and feet. Both men suffered horrendous head injuries.

After the killings, the *coup de grace* was that one (certainly 'crazy man' Jackman) or more extensively urinated over the deceased.

Jackman, who traded in fear, demanded bottles of beer be fetched while his evil henchman, Esposito, paced around the blood-drenched room planning their next move. The merciless beasts decided to flee, and went as far as London in a desperate bid to escape the law – but before setting off they contemplated setting fire to the flat to destroy any evidence.

During the court case, *Infinity* nightclub worker Joanne Martlew told how the killers 'disappeared' just hours after the murder, in Esposito's uncle's Mercedes van. The trio drove to Ormskirk then Skelmersdale where Sammon was dropped off before he returned to Southport to get his blooded clothes and training shoes washed. The other two, after abandoning the van at Knutsford, Cheshire, got a train from Manchester to London. Lying low in 'the Smoke' they booked in to a bed and breakfast near Euston Station, while a massive manhunt for the perpetrators gathered pace. They returned to Southport early the next morning.

Meanwhile, Mr MacElhinney returned to his flat in the early hours, around 7.30 am and made the gruesome discovery – his friends' bloodstained bodies in his bedsit. They were lying in close proximity face down slumped by the couch in the main room. Hagan was slumped over the sofa and Perry was in the foetal position by the settee. Both had enormous, multiple head injuries, sustaining a total of eighteen serious head injuries and many other insults. Paramedics had responded to an anonymous 999 call made at 7.33 am. The full horror of the crime then unfolded.

At about 7.40 am the police were alerted to the blood-drenched scene and the area, involving two semi-detached houses, were cordoned off with police tape, and forensic officers arrived fifteen minutes later to begin a painstaking finger-tip search. The ground-floor flat (No1) of 6 Derby Road, had become a major crime scene and before long, a large pack of regional and national media converged on the roadway.

Christopher Lloyd, a forensic scientist, said the flat was covered in blood, particularly on and at the side of the bed where he believed the two men were attacked before moving nearer the settee area. Some attempt had been made to dispose of part of the incrimination evidence, in bin bags, but forensic evidence clearly linked the three defendants to the bloodbath scene.

The heavily-blooded and bent baseball bat was recovered from the scene and forensically examined, it was obviously the main murder weapon as was a bloodstained knife.

The flats were owned by local landlord Antonio Biondi, who was a relative of Esposito – who did not pay him rent, but helped with

Manhunt in Derby Road. The murder scene is searched by experts. Southportgb.com

The two bodies are removed from the murder scene. Southportgb.com

odd jobs, including collecting money from other tenants. Jimmy had lived in the flat for about eight months.

The *Southport Visiter* – the first on the scene – was told by crime officers how two men had been found. At 3 pm the victims' bodies were removed from the scene of devastation.

Dr Brian Rodgera, the Home Office pathologist, conducted post-mortems which officially revealed both men died from severe head injuries, caused by a blunt instrument; one of the men also had injuries consistent with having defended himself. Both men had extensive injuries to their faces, arms, legs and back. Tests were carried out to see if drugs were present in the victims' systems, although there were no illegal drugs on the premises.

Paul Hagan had suffered twelve head injuries, 'typical of blunt force trauma,' causing massive bleeding of the scalp with underlying haemorrhage and several skull fractures. He had eight bruises on his back consistent with impact with a baseball bat, his left testicle had suffered major trauma and he had defensive

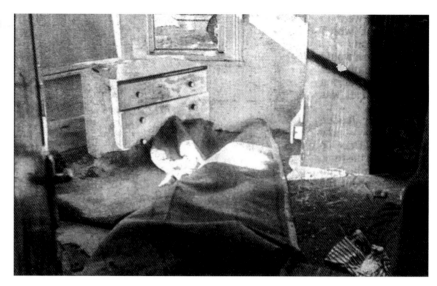

Two interior shots of the murder house in Derby Road, showing the devastation that was caused by the murderers. Southport Champion

wounds showing he had not died immediately. Mr Perry had twenty-eight major lacerations to his head and neck resulting in extensive haemorrhaging and massive skull damage, his head driven down into his spine.

On the Thursday, 20 June, Merseyside Police officially launched a murder hunt.

Raffaele Esposito gave himself up the day after the murder, walking into Southport Police Station at 5.15 pm, with his solicitor. He was charged with murder, although denied killing the two Huyton men. Investigating officer DC Asher described him as 'wary' throughout the interview. During the interrogation he declined to comment on any questions put to him, and in fact, maintained this silence until his court trial. Later the same day Sean Jackman was arrested at his Portland Street home, where he'd lived for four years. Sammon,

Esposito's murdering henchman, Sean Jackman.
Southport Visiter

arrested the following day, appeared in court on 26 June and was remanded with the other two for trial. DS Kerruish said:

> *This was a savage, brutal attack on two young men who had everything to live for. It has shocked the whole community. They were known to the police but I don't think that has any relevance to the case.*

The police were obviously anxious to talk to a number of people who lived in the same block of flats – but some hadn't been seen since the grisly incidents.

Neighbours were shocked to learn of the murders, but claimed the area already had a bad reputation, especially a drugs problem; several said it was just a matter of time before something like this happened. One resident heard shouting around 11 pm, but that wasn't unusual. There had been a scuffle a few weeks previously in one of the flats and the ground floor window of the 'murder flat' had been smashed twice in one day.

Reports of noise – banging and shouting – from the flat were heard about 1.30 am, and again during the early hours, and then there was a violent argument and three much reported loud bangs about 3 am. One witness said it sounded pretty violent, like someone kicking a door in – but because it was a regular occurrence it was ignored.

A man waiting for a lift to his farm job, at 4.15 am, heard loud noises, banging and smashing sounds coming from within the flat, as well as shouting and swearing. He could hear a man crying and then moaning and groaning. The noise became very loud and he became scared. A passing cyclist, who knew Esposito and Jackman, bravely looked through a gap in the curtains and saw them arguing. Half an hour later, at about 4.45 am, Sammon got a taxi to the *Scarisbrick Hotel*. Two hours later another taxi driver saw all three men talking together in Hoghton Street. One Derby Road resident said:

> The area has gone from bad to worse. There are plenty of decent folk around here, but there is also a bad element. It's not unusual to see police cars around but two deaths is a shock.

Detectives originally had no motive, so the attacks were shrouded in mystery until the investigation got going, led by Detective Superintendent John Kerruish. After speaking to people who had seen the victims out drinking, the motive became apparent – the sole reason for the deaths was Esposito's jealousy. Detective Inspector Reily said:

> I thought it was odd that this attack was so ferocious over something so minor. But Esposito's jealousy was the only possible motive, although we have never known the exact sequence of events in that flat that day or who dealt what blows.

A killer profile of Sean Michael Jackman, revealed that he was one of the resort's most notorious characters, heralded as 'the hardest man in Southport'. The thirty-three-year old, near twenty-stone keen bodybuilder, had been a nightclub doorman for a decade. He was also a lifeguard at Southport Baths for six years and worked for a loans company. When he was twenty-two years old he was hauled before the courts and given a conditional discharge for common assault, and being drunk and disorderly. He claimed: 'Southport was his and everything that went on went on through him.'

Raffaele Esposito, of Derby Road, formerly of Truscott Road,

Burscough, was a twenty-five-year-old doorman and a former licensee of *Bar Forino's*, in Eastbank Street. Known as 'Raff,' this 5ft 2in bodybuilder was, pure and simply, a callous and vicious thug.

One-time friend of Esposito, twenty-four-year-old Joseph Edward Sammon, of Banastre Road – known as 'Joey' – was the third member. A self-employed plumber by day, he was known to be 'hard,' although had no criminal background. He worked on the door at *The Carlton Hotel* and *G-Spot* nightclubs.

Esposito, Jackman and Sammon, stood side-by-side when they appeared at North Sefton Magistrates' Court for the first time on Monday, 24 June 2002, charged with murder. During the thirty-four minute hearing defence solicitors argued for bail. Esposito's father offered to put up a surety of £2,500 for his son's bail, but magistrate's bench chairman, Mr Len Mann, after deliberating for fourteen minutes, refused the grant application. The men then remained in custody until their appearance in Liverpool on Tuesday, 2 July.

The Southport hearing had attracted a strong police presence with armed officers strategically placed in the packed courtroom where the families of both the victims and suspects sat. Six uniformed officers and three detectives were in the courtroom while four uniformed officers were positioned in the court's upper gallery. A skirmish broke out after magistrates had retired to consider bail applications. Two members of the public were involved in a minor scuffle inside the court foyer, but the police quickly dealt with the fracas and no-one was arrested.

Cowardly killer, Sean Jackman, tried to escape justice by controversially marrying his girlfriend inside Altcourse Prison on 18 November, the day before his murder trial began, to the fury of police and the Crown Prosecution Service. The wedding meant Amanda (Mandy) Brunskill, who Jackman had confessed his guilt to in a telephone conversation, could not then be forced to give evidence against him, by law. Because wives do not have to give prosecution evidence against their husbands, the police feared the case would collapse, the press were banned from reporting anything about the marriage and now, Mrs Jackman couldn't even be referred to in court.

However, the rest of the evidence was compelling enough. The trio appeared at Liverpool Crown Court on 2 July, and then on 10 September, when they all pleaded not guilty to the murders.

The Crown Court murder trial began on Monday, 18 November, but three days later the case collapsed, after suddenly being halted and the jury discharged, because one of the accused, Esposito, had dismissed his barrister. With a second jury sworn in the trial resumed on Wednesday, 27 November, in a packed Crown Court, and lasted over three weeks.

The prosecuting QC was Jonathan Foster. The prosecution's case was that Esposito had been summoned to the Derby Road flat where Paul Hagan and Francis Perry were proving troublesome to the two girls. He had received a 'phone call at 2.30 am from his girlfriend', after she had gone back to the house with Perry and Hagan. He in turn 'summoned his troops,' recruiting Jackman to his cause and in due course, Sammon.

When Esposito and Jackman got to the flat, about 3 am, the two men were in MacElhinney's flat, extremely drunk. Esposito's sister and girlfriend were in an upstairs flat, and he said they were cagey and upset. Eventually his sister said Perry 'had got a bit over friendly with his hands'. Esposito admitted attacking Mr Perry, having lost self-control, but maintained he did not kill the two men, but merely assaulted them, adding:

> *He had his hands all over my girlfriend and when she asked him to take his hands off he would not. She became scared and ran out the room. On hearing this I lost my temper completely. I picked up a baseball bat and assaulted him with it. I beat him up and down the right side of his body, his arms, legs, rib cage and back. Rage had got the better of me.*

Esposito again went on to describe how he and Jackman rained blows on Mr Perry's face, arms, legs and groin, stamped on his groin and kicked his face – then they turned their attention to Mr Hagan with the bat, and eventually left both men on the floor. Esposito said he was extremely drunk and adrenaline was running high. He then began to panic and rang Sammon, who agreed to go round to the flat.

At this juncture the sordid tale becomes a bit fuzzy, with Sammon giving one version of events, and Esposito and Jackman trying to pass the buck claiming it was Sammon – and not them – who struck the final and fatal blows.

The co-accused, Joey Sammon, had decided to give evidence against Jackman and Esposito after they conspired to set him up for murder.

Esposito attempted to get Jackman off the hook by saying he arrived after the victims had died – and blamed Sammon for inflicting the final killer blows, saying they were still conscious and talking when Sammon repeatedly hit them with a gas bottle, the baseball bat and then kicked and punched them, to 'finish the job'.

Esposito said he decided to go back to the flat to explain his behavior, and found Mr Perry sitting on the bed and Mr Hagan on the sofa. They were so drunk they did not seem to know what had happened to them. 'I did not apologise but told them why I had done it.' They became abusive and telling me to get out. He alleged that Hagan told Perry that they should come back and shoot Esposito and Sammon – who didn't take that well and lost his head, picked up a calor gas bottle from the hallway, lifted it above his head and hit Mr Perry across the shoulders while he was on the bed shouting 'who do you think you are?' He added:

Sammon hit both men with the bottle, before picking up the bat. He had been drinking and was clearly off his head. He had also been taking cocaine that night. He then gave the pair a good kicking that went on for about five minutes – and came to an end when he took a swing at one of their heads. I said don't hit them around the head and he stopped and started shouting at them.

Esposito claimed the two men were still conscious and talking when Sammon arrived and battered them, and that he had only hit them a few times, 'before Joey went berserk and killed them'. He said he went back upstairs to the girls, and then heard sounds of screaming and banging from the downstairs flat and Sammon shouting; when he got there both victims were lying motionless. They were dead.

Jackman's QC was Charles Chruszcz. Jackman originally said he did not see the deceased in the nightclub and went home at 2 am, sleeping until 11 am. He later claimed the two victims were already dead by the time he arrived, and that Sammon repeatedly hit them long after they died. But Sammon shouted from the dock: 'How can you lie like that? I cannot understand how you can do it to me.' The judge warned Sammon that if there were any more outbursts he would be taken to the cells.

Sean Jackman said he had walked round to Esposito's flat after having an argument with his girlfriend and been locked out of his Portland Street house for drinking and taking cocaine. When he got there he claimed he was greeted by a bloodbath and a shocked Esposito, who was 'very white and in shock'. He said: 'You've got to help me, look in here.' And there were two dead men. Raff was in a state he said: 'Joey's killed them, having gone berserk.'

He denied his 'hardest' reputation saying: 'That is absolute rubbish – I am a big bloke but I would not class myself as a hard man.' He said he had been wearing a grey bomber-jacket and sweat shirt that night, but took off his shirt and T-shirt because they had splattered blood on and he didn't want any connection with the incident, although he admitting helping to 'tidy up' the flat where wet blood was widely distributed and put stuff in bin bags and moved things around.

Sammons' QC, David Aubrey, described Esposito's 'made up story' as 'Alice in Wonderland' stuff, adding: 'This killing had already been set up. It is a fantasy from start to finish.'

Right from the start Joseph Sammon said he had absolutely no connection with the murders at all, and denied being involved in any physical violence. He said he went to the *West End Club* to look for a friend who owed him £1,000 but she was not there and so he returned home to his girlfriend, Kelly, about 2.30 am. Half an hour later Esposito rang him, panicking. He said: 'We need you, something has happened.' They wanted him to drive round in his van but it had a puncture so he got a taxi round.

Sammon said he 'went along' because he was terrified of 'sick in the head' Jackman – he said 'everyone in Southport knows Sean is violent. People do things because they are very scared of him. Everyone socializes with him for the wrong reasons.'

Esposito let him into the flat where he saw Jackman and Esposito's sister and girlfriend. After the girls left, Sammon asked Esposito what was going on. He replied: 'We've done two lads in and need a van to get rid of them.' Sammon said that when he arrived at the flat the two men were already dead on the floor, but 'paranoid' Jackman still kept 'laying into' the bodies shouting: 'What's wrong with his head?' Jackman was convinced they were still alive.

Sammon added: 'I could tell Raff didn't want to do what Sean was saying. I was in the hall and I heard thumps and I was just shouting "please stop". But Sean replied: "Are you with us or them?" He kept saying things like: "Do you want a go?" but I said no way, and he added: "Who's side is everyone on?" Sean turned to Raff and said: "It's your call" and I said: "There's nothing to call, they are dead – look at them." Sammon added:

There is no way I killed them. I get flashbacks, at night when I try and sleep I get pictures of certain things. It is just sick, it shouldn't have happened. There was no need to end their lives in a sick and violent way, they were two healthy men. Sean said to me that I was in it as much as they were. I just wanted to go home. If I had tried to get the baseball bat out of his hand he would have killed me as well. I was told I had to run off with them because I had seen too much. I didn't go to the police because I was very scared. I was frightened to death.

Sammon said the other two had both taken drugs, and that Jackman was fuming because he had not brought his van; he then gave Sammon £20 to buy beer. He got a taxi to the *Scarisbrick Hotel* and stayed for a drink. A former *Scarisbrick Hotel* night manager, Anthony White, told the court he saw Sammon walk into the hotel reception in the early morning of 19 June, between 4 am and 5 am, looking 'shaken' and wipe blood off his hands, which in his opinion was not his own blood.

When he returned to the flat Jackman, who had speckles of blood on his face, quickly drank one of the bottles of beer. He saw the bodies of the two men and realized he was standing in a pool of blood. He was then ordered to get a van belonging to Esposito's uncle. While out fetching petrol for the van, he called at the home of his girlfriend, Mrs Samantha Lowe, about 6 am and told her that he had seen 'dreadful things' and that the other two had beaten up two men. She saw he had blood splattered on his trousers, above his knee and on his trainers.

Sammons girlfriend said he was a gentle man who she hoped to settle down with, and denied, during cross-examination, that she was suffering from love blindness.

Joseph Sammon left her house and was waiting for a taxi when the two men drove by in another taxi and stopped for him, saying they were going to London and made him get into the back of the van. En-route Jackman kept expressing doubts about Sammon but Sammon assured them he would not contact the police so they let him out of the van at Skelmersdale.

The double murder trial blew the top off the secrecy which surrounds Southport's drugs underworld. Throughout the trial allegations were made about nightspots in town which it was claimed Esposito, Jackman and Sammon used to sell hard drugs. Jackman brought cocaine in from Liverpool while Esposito cut it up and bagged it in a flat above Forino's club where he was licensee. They used a taxi driver to deliver the drugs to customers.

Sammon said his life was a mess after March because of a major row with his girlfriend in Tenerife, after which he stabbed himself in the stomach. Asked by his barrister David Aubrey QC if rumours that he was a major drugs supplier were true, replied 'rubbish'. However, he later admitted that he got involved in drugs in the troublesome March. He broke down in tears when giving evidence claiming the other two had been drug dealers for years. Sammon said he had never touched drugs or been involved with them before March that year. He then started to smoke cannabis and use cocaine and helped the other two men supply drugs.

Mr Justice Royce reminded the jury of evidence put before them during the case. He pointed to DNA tests carried out on the deceased as well as testimony from a forensic scientist who detailed how blood found at the scene fell into different categories, including airborne blood, and visible blood, adding:

The baseball bat was heavily bloodstained and the handle was bent. These were all expert witnesses and they are entitled to express their opinions but you must take into account the evidence of the defence and what they say.

After the judge had summed up the case (19 December) the jury retired to deliberate and consider their verdict. On 20 December

2002, after deliberating for six hours, the jury of eight women and four men returned a unanimous verdict of 'guilty' to convict Esposito and Jackman, on two charges of murder. Neither men showed any emotion when the jury pronounced them guilty. Before sentencing, Jon Benson, QC, defending Esposito, said that he had no previous convictions and there was nothing to suggest he was a danger to the public. Imposing a life sentence for each murder, the judge added:

> *These were brutal, callous and vicious murders. The deceased men were begging for their lives and you showed no mercy. There is only one sentence – life in each case.*

Jackman and Esposito were led to the cells surrounded by seven dock security officers. There was also extra security in court with nine guards and uniformed police officers strategically placed in the courtroom. As the convicted killers were taken away, supporters of the victims shouted out abuse including, 'bastards, rot in hell'.

The two families attended every day of the trial and were relieved when Jackman and Esposito were sent down. But their relief turned to disbelief.

The jury, who had needed a further hour's deliberation on Sammon's involvement, gave a majority direction that found him 'not guilty'. Sammon, who had been kept apart in prison and in the dock from his co-accused for his own safety, was therefore acquitted, cleared.

The victims' families and friends, including some members of the jury, burst into tears or wept quietly as the verdict was read out; some were horrified and walked out in disgust at the verdict, while others shouted and stormed out of the public gallery hurling angry abuse at the jury members: 'That is f...ing disgusting, I hope you can sleep,' shouted one and another yelled: 'He never helped two dying men, you should be ashamed of yourself.'

Mr Perry's thirty-eight-year-old sister, Paula, wished to thank people who helped put Jackman and Esposito behind bars, said:

> *We cannot tell you how pleased we are that these two animals are off the streets. They have ruined our families' lives and they deserve what they got for killing our Buddy. The people of Southport have been*

fantastic and we would like to say a big thank you to everyone who came and gave evidence against them. We know how hard it must have been but we are very grateful.

Another of Mr Perry's sisters, Joanne, added:

Buddy and Paul were two of a kind, they meant nobody any harm. We all loved them. It is just disgusting what they did to them. Jackman was a timebomb who was waiting to go off. Esposito just stood there in the dock and lied, they make me sick. Having to sit in the same room as them, they are just evil savages, but at least the world is a better place now.

The senior investigating officer, DS John Kerruish, said after the case:

I am pleased with the decision of the court and that both men face long sentences for committing what was an extremely violent crime. Paul and Francis suffered a maintained and vicious attack and their injuries were extensive. We may never know exactly what took place in the early hours of that Wednesday morning, or the full reason why this attack happened. However, Jackman and Esposito have been brought to bear for the brutal crime that they committed. This attack was rigorously investigated by a dedicated team of Merseyside Police officers. I would like to thank them for their hard work which has resulted in this conviction. Our thoughts remain at this time with Paul and Francis' families. We hope that this verdict will allow the relatives and friends of both men to try and rebuild their lives and begin to try to come to terms with their loss.

The *Southport Visiter's* editorial lead comment on 27 December, was:

Murderers Sean Jackman and Raffaele Esposito were lucky this week – they sat down to a Christmas dinner. Their victims Paul Hagan and Francis Perry were not so lucky. At this time for family, peace and harmony, your heart goes out to the dead mens' families who will never see their loved ones again. The only consolation as they meet Jackman and Esposito's chilling, emotionless stares in today's Visiter is knowing they will not walk the streets again for a very long time. Justice has prevailed but that will come as cold comfort for the Hagans and the Perrys. The family wanted to thank you, the people of Southport, for coming together as a community to help bring the two killers to justice.

The horror flat that had been described as a scene of 'devastation and death,' was shortly taken over – including others in the block – by a church group, who said the flats were to be used as part of a 'positive project to aid those without shelter'. Three properties were let to Pastor Peter Cunningham, of Argyle Road Church, who then rented out the refurbished and decorated flats as part of his long term quest to help Southport's homeless, and re-home the under-privileged. They were originally leased by Mr Biondi, and later bought outright. The church leader said his dream target was to accumulate 300 properties in Southport which would house the needy people in the resort who had nowhere to call home. This latest purchase brought his tally up to fifty-two. He added:

Two different photographs of the two murder victims, Francis Perry and Paul Hagan, both from Huyton. Champion newspaper

These properties in Derby Road are known for their problem status, but they have now come into the ownership of Green Pastures who help the homeless and poor. We want to turn the flats into a place of harmony and rid it of the turmoil. A lot of the people we look after are not always the type to be able to go out to work. Some of them are drug addicts or alcoholics who need help and support. Our plan is to run it for a variety of people who have different needs.

The initial attack was designed to cause maximum pain and humiliation; the ultimate plan was to kill. The powerful bouncers armed themselves in advance, and there was evidence of sadism, gratuitous violence, sexual maltreatment and degradation of the victims – who had been on their knees begging to be spared.

The trial judge called it 'a truly terrible case', and said the 'tariff' on their life terms must be that they spend 19 years as 'two life sentences' each, which means they could serve as much as 30 years behind bars.

The Scarisbrick Hotel, *Lord Street.* Author's collection

Bibliography

Primary Sources
Southport Visiter (various issues)
Southport Star
Southport Champion
Liverpool Daily Post
The Independent, July 3, 1999. Article by Jason Bennetto.

Secondary Sources
Bland, Edward, *Annals of Southport* (1903)
Darwin, Sgt. Charles A, *Southport County Bor. Police* 1870-1969 (1969)
Fielding, Steve, *Lancashire Tales of Mystery & Murder* (2003)
Greenwood, Cedric, *Thatch, Towers and Colonnades* (1971)
Johnson, Keith, *Chilling True Tales of Old Lancashire* (2000)
Jones, Steve, *Lancashire Lasses* (2001)
Lane, Brian, *The Murder Guide* (1991)
Wetsch, Elizabeth, *Dr Clements* (Internet 2005)
Wright, Geoff, *Southport Visiter* article (Nov 1992)
Wright, Geoff, *Southport: A Century Ago* (1992)

Index

*(Numbers in **bold** represent illustrations)*

Subjects and Places